John Cassavetes: Interviews

Conversations with Filmmakers Series
Gerald Peary, General Editor

John Cassavetes
INTERVIEWS

Edited by Gabriella Oldham

University Press of Mississippi / Jackson

www.upress.state.ms.us

The University Press of Mississippi is a member of the Association of American University Presses.

Copyright © 2016 by University Press of Mississippi
All rights reserved
Manufactured in the United States of America

First printing 2016

Library of Congress Cataloging-in-Publication Data

Names: Cassavetes, John, 1929–1989 author. | Oldham, Gabriella, editor.
Title: John Cassavetes : interviews / edited by Gabriella Oldham.
Description: Jackson : University Press of Mississippi, 2016. | Series:
    Conversations with filmmakers series | Includes bibliographical references
    and index. | Description based on print version record and CIP data
    provided by publisher; resource not viewed.
Identifiers: LCCN 2016019885 (print) | LCCN 2016010732 (ebook) | ISBN
    9781496806703 (epub single) | ISBN 9781496806710 (epub institutional) |
    ISBN 9781496806727 (pdf single) | ISBN 9781496806734 (pdf institutional)
    | ISBN 9781496806697 (hardcover : alk. paper)
Subjects: LCSH: Cassavetes, John, 1929–1989—Interviews. | Motion picture
    actors and actresses—United States—Interviews. | Motion picture
    producers and directors—United States—Interviews. | Independent
    filmmakers—United States—Interviews.
Classification: LCC PN1998.3.C384 (print) | LCC PN1998.3.C384 A3 2016 (ebook)
    | DDC 791.4302/33092—dc23
LC record available at https://lccn.loc.gov/2016019885

British Library Cataloging-in-Publication Data available

Contents

Introduction

Maverick. Non-conformist. Angry young man. Accidental genius. Gray eminence of American independent moviemakers. Everyman. These and other labels have been bestowed on filmmaker John Cassavetes. His body of work as an independent director totaled only nine personal films made over a little more than twenty-five years, but they impacted the cinema culture of the 1960s to the 1980s in unprecedented ways. His filmmaking style and content both mesmerized and rankled critics and audiences in the US while finding a warmer critical embrace in Europe. Yet in both parts of the world, cineastes elevated him to near-cult status for his cinematic vision and perspective.

This across-the-spectrum reception led Cassavetes during his lifetime to exude an aura of feisty contradiction about him. His unapologetic disdain of Hollywood as anti-creative and anti-artist was his source of pride and badge of courage at a time when he felt directors meekly followed studio command. Yet Cassavetes the actor made good use of Hollywood films to pay the bills for his personal projects. Fascinated by the complexity of human relationships, Cassavetes sought to capture these nuances in his multifaceted portraits of "average" men and women. Yet he also displayed occasional sexist, at times exaggerated characterizations. As a director devoted to the actor, Cassavetes intently believed in the actors' unrestricted potential to explore raw emotional depth, creating a perception of improvisational freedom. Yet most of his lengthy scripts were in fact personally dictated, fully detailed, and tightly structured. Finally, Cassavetes now dwells in the pantheon of iconoclastic filmmakers from an era of cinematic soul-searching and creative turbulence. Yet he was overlooked and underacknowledged for his cinematic contributions for many years. In an overdue portrait of a man of extremes in his own words, this collection of interviews and articles featuring John Cassavetes during his life, from 1958 to 1984 (plus a "lost" interview that appeared online in 2009), offers new insight into his growth as an actor, his evolution as a filmmaker, and his staunch advocacy of artistic freedom.

To trace this portrait, one can pinpoint four prominent themes that filter throughout and unify these publications. The first theme is Cassavetes's identity as an independent filmmaker—what he considered his raison d'être. In asserting his independence, Cassavetes demonstrated another core contradiction: he lambasted and dropped people and structures that seemed bent on curtailing his expressive freedom, yet remained fiercely loyal to and supported those who fueled his independence. His individualistic and cynical streak pushed him to speak his mind, often bluntly, even crassly, about what was wrong with Hollywood and, of course, the world itself. Yet his statements included almost child-like admissions of a belief in humanity's better self—a self that could possibly save the world through artistic creativity.

This segues into the second prominent theme of Cassavetes's beliefs and views, and the personal relationships that molded his films. His own frustration at running into brick walls as an artist was tempered by a surprising naïveté that he transferred to his characters, both male and female. Because his family and co-workers were his refuge in an angry world, Cassavetes could channel his high energy through storytelling and through the people he trusted to enact those stories. With long-time associates on his productions and his core acting ensemble, including his wife Gena Rowlands, in-laws, parents, and young children, Cassavetes found an intuitive acceptance of his vision. At the same time, in another inevitable contradiction, Cassavetes's vision was sometimes so intense and bewildering, he mentioned in an interview with Michael Ventura that Rowlands once exclaimed to him, "Who the hell can understand you?! You're nuts!"

The third theme then can be lifted out of Cassavetes's position in the physical world among his family and colleagues and into the emotional world of his films. His main exploration was human nature, which in the majority of his films was distilled specifically to men-women relationships. Cassavetes's unrelenting camera lens documented the characters' emotional dysfunctions bordering on abuse; he watched as they reacted with primal instincts to ordinary circumstances, surviving their brutality and accepting each other's flaws and limitations. While fascinated by men's behaviors which he examined repeatedly with cronies Peter Falk, Ben Gazzara, and Seymour Cassel, Cassavetes was especially smitten with depicting the soul of women, many of whom were personified by Gena Rowlands. He built his stories around her ability to express degrees of living and feeling—passion, resignation, insanity, innocence, fury—without recoiling from the vulnerability her roles exposed. As an ensemble director, Cassavetes explored success, failure, resilience, and existence in a middle-class world, drawing both from what he observed and what he knew his actors could bring to the set.

Because he recognized the unlimited resources that actors could offer him, and because of his own intense work as a television and film actor, Cassavetes the director felt compelled to let his actors unleash their potentials, shape their own cinematic realities, and play them out naturally on the screen—thus his reputation as an "actor's director." This fourth theme not only zeroes in on his working method with actors, but also on his overall technical film style that he considered subservient—often intrusive—to the actors' needs. Cassavetes's cinematography and editing techniques often created a film-viewing experience for the audience that mirrored the emotional chaos depicted onscreen. Using his camera as a kind of fly-on-the-wall, Cassavetes participated in a hand-held pursuit of the characters moving in or out of frame, or through languishing, seemingly endless close-ups of raw emotional reality. His scriptwriting as well, often considered sketchy and improvisational because of the spontaneous camerawork or random (i.e., "unedited") feel of the scenes, was in fact structured carefully from the outset, but allowed unlimited flexibility for the actors to animate their characters. For Cassavetes, all of these threads—his independence, his support network, his philosophy of life, and his cinematic language—ultimately converged to create a small but powerful set of films linked by his need to express an artistic vision of what it means to be human.

Cassavetes initially had no inclination to direct; for him, acting was a channel for his own wild, prankish personality and love of control and independence. In fact, Cassavetes was more intrigued by the prospect of meeting women than studying acting when he enrolled in the American Academy of Dramatic Arts in New York. He nonetheless built on his experiences and recognized the importance of the actors' craft as he began to work on live television in rebellious, loner, outcast roles. When he co-founded his own acting workshop with Burton Lane in 1957 to help struggling actors hone their training, Cassavetes drew on his rebellious leadership qualities which many found charismatic, magnetic, and supportive. At the same time, he was the first to admit not knowing what he was doing as an acting teacher and yielded to his "students'" unlimited explorations of character and storytelling through improvisation. From the Cassavetes-Lane Theatre Workshop came the genesis of his first personal film, *Shadows*.

Early on during his television jobs and interactions with network powers, Cassavetes questioned and rapidly shunned the profit motive and corporate strangleholds on artistic freedom. These conflicts would remain a thorn in Cassavetes's side that he repeatedly griped about in interviews. In a 1975 interview with Judith McNally, when reflecting on the question "Can a picture make 100 million?" Cassavetes responded, "Who the hell cares? If you're thinking that way, you're not making films, you're making money. If that's what it's come to, let the audience look at pictures of money. . . ." In addition to interviews as a forum for his philosophy of independence in a money-driven business, Cassavetes wrote his own essays in the trade papers expounding on the failure of Hollywood to understand true creativity. Despite his love of actors, it was not beyond Cassavetes to point his finger at them for compromising and betraying their beliefs. This dilemma was exceedingly familiar to Cassavetes who willingly accepted roles as an actor in some none-too-artistic films expressly for paychecks that he, in turn, cashed to pay off his personal projects. This choice, however, was made in the full knowledge that when he finished his noncreative jobs, Cassavetes's homemade, out-of-pocket-funded films would represent his true artistic expression. Even if it meant mortgaging his house and spending four years on one film, he recognized independent filmmaking as his resistance to being swallowed by a callous business. His freedom was not without costs to his career; during the early sixties, after challenging, criticizing, and insulting one too many movie bigwig, Cassavetes was blackballed and could only find sporadic roles while he stayed home to garden and babysit his children as Rowlands worked.

Despite his setbacks, Cassavetes never stopped inventing new opportunities and stories—the low points were only catapults on a springboard into professional satisfaction. By trailblazing an independent route to his personal artistic success when few other filmmakers did, Cassavetes eventually balanced sleeping with the devil with exorcizing it single-handedly. In multiple interviews, his thoughts on the topic of artistic freedom were directed at both ruthless producers and artists who would not seek alternative creative options. As he wrote in his *Film Culture* essay as early as 1959: "Without individual creative expression, we are left with a medium of irrelevant fantasies that can add nothing but slim diversion to an already diversified world. . . . Only by allowing the artist full and free creative expression will the art and the business of motion pictures survive." Vehemently upholding this view for the rest of his life, Cassavetes became the consummate filmmaker—writer, actor, director, camera operator, producer, distributor, spokesman, and inspiration for young filmmakers of the seventies.

When Cassavetes died in 1989 at the age of fifty-nine, critical reflections on his life and work continued to stress the paradoxes of his legacy. For a man who affirmed in a 1980 interview for the *Los Angeles Times* that "I'm not a maverick. I just like to make movies," Janet Maslin in the *New York Times* in 1989 questioned such a simple statement in her assessment: "He did not make films that were easily categorized, easily analyzed or even, for most audiences, easily liked." In its obituary for Cassavetes, *People* called him "Everyman as filmmaker," but added, "You can never be sure whether what you're seeing is artful or artless." It is perhaps his Everyman image that most emblemizes his independent work and has triggered a new cycle of rediscovery for Cassavetes, who for many years after his death was relegated to a footnote in modern film history. Audiences remain uneasily seduced by the emotional rawness of his filmmaking, transfixed by its chaotic order (and orderly chaos), and even nostalgic for a time when an individual's passion refused to fit into a preset mold.

Long unavailable, five of Cassavetes's most important films were released in

2004 as a boxed DVD set, which Manohla Dargis in the *New York Times* called "a must-have fetish item." The title of that review was aptly called "John Cassavetes, Laughing Last." With this new volume of published interviews with a unique filmmaker, Cassavetes's spirit of contradiction is once more unleashed—and that would probably please him no end.

Special thanks to:

The many who helped research and grant permissions for the articles included in this book: Jean Curnyn (*TV Guide*); Jovita Dominguez (Directors Guild of America); Martin Gibbs (London News Syndication); Lisa Lebowitz (Variety Media LLC); Heidi Marshall (Columbia College Chicago); Mike Pepin (American Film Institute); Erik Piil (Anthology Film Archives); Angelo Russo and Anthony Puterio (*New York Daily News*); Jessica Stremmel (The YGS Group); Erica Varela (*Los Angeles Times*); and Rob Winter (British Film Institute).

The interviewers and authors (or the relatives thereof) whose devotion to John Cassavetes from the time they met until today remains steadfast, enthusiastic, and generously supportive of this book to keep his legacy alive: Dan Adler (for Dick Adler), Dolores Barclay, Gautam Dasgupta, Ken Gross (for Larry Gross), Joe Leydon, Jonas Mekas, Sheila Zinser Rogoff (for Jesse Zunser), Deac Rossell, and Michael Ventura.

Kristine Krueger at the National Film Information Service, Margaret Herrick Library, Academy of Motion Picture Arts and Sciences for her assistance in locating articles.

Paul Rossi for his excellent translations of two articles from *Positif*.

John Crittenden for photographing John Cassavetes with such sensitivity and allowing his work to grace the cover.

Valerie Jones at University Press of Mississippi for her great attention to detail, follow-up, and humor in helping with permissions, photographs, and the minutiae of publishing.

Leila Salisbury at University Press of Mississippi for her ongoing guidance, patience, and support of this volume.

This book is dedicated to I.O., who often said I was the spirit of contradiction.

GO

Chronology

1929   John Nicholas Cassavetes born December 9 in New York City of parents Nicholas John and Katherine; lived in Greece for his early years and returned to New York at the age of seven speaking no English.

1949–50   Transfers from Colgate University to attend American Academy of Dramatic Arts, New York.

1954   Breakout role as bullfighter in Budd Schulberg's "Paso Doble" for NBC's *Omnibus*. Marries Gena Rowlands on March 19 in New York City; she along with other family members would star in most of his later personal films. Three children follow: Nick (1959), Alexandra (1965), and Zoe (1970).

1954–57   Appears in more than ninety live dramatic television shows.

1955–59   Film roles in *The Night Holds Terror* (1955), *Crime in the Streets* (1956), *Saddle the Wind* (1958), *Virgin Island* (1959).

1957   First starring role in *Edge of the City* with Sidney Poitier, in addition to short theatrical tours. Also starts Cassavetes-Lane Theatre Workshop in New York (with Burton Lane) to help struggling actors practice their craft; workshops include improvisations that lead to his first film *Shadows*.

1958   Holds three midnight shows of *Shadows* at Paris Theatre in New York to mostly negative response, with some effusive exceptions (Henry Jaglom, Jonas Mekas of *Film Culture*).

1959   Stars as *Johnny Staccato* on NBC and later ABC for less than one season (twenty-seven out of thirty-nine episodes) before parting ways with network; also directs five episodes. Releases reshot/re-edited version of *Shadows*.

1960   *Shadows* chosen by British Film Institute for Beat, Square, and Cool Festival; wins award at Venice Film Festival.

1960–65   Appears in and/or directs episodes of *Rawhide*, *The Lloyd Bridges Show*, *Breaking Point*, *The Legend of Jesse James*, and *Combat!*

1961   Shows second "official" version of *Shadows* at Embassy Theatre in New York to mixed reviews tempered by critical excitement over the raw depiction of real people.

1962   Writes (with Richard Capp) and directs *Too Late Blues* for Paramount; receives seven-year nonexclusive contract as director.

1962–65   Directs *A Child Is Waiting*; parts ways with Paramount, leading to several years of being "blackballed" in Hollywood and staying at home to garden and raise kids, with occasional theatrical appearances.

1967   Stars in *The Killers*, originally made for NBC TV but deemed too violent and released in theaters.

1968   Writes, directs, and produces *Faces*, which he shoots at his own house; featured at New York Film Festival. Among other awards and nominations (in 1969): Venice Film Festival Awards (Best Film, Best Actor [John Marley]) and nomination for Gold Lion (Cassavetes); National Society of Film Critics Awards (USA) for Best Screenplay (Cassavetes) and Best Supporting Actor (Seymour Cassel); Academy Award Nominations (Best Writing, Story, Screenplay [Cassavetes], Best Supporting Actor [Seymour Cassel], Best Supporting Actress [Lynn Carlin]). Stars in *Dirty Dozen* (dir. Robert Altman) for which Cassavetes receives Oscar nomination for Best Supporting Actor. Stars in *Rosemary's Baby* (dir. Roman Polanski) and *Machine Gun McCain* (dir. Giuliano Montaldo).

1970   Writes, directs, and acts in *Husbands* with Peter Falk and Ben Gazzara (screenplay by Cassavetes is nominated for 1971 Golden Globe Award).

1971   Writes and directs *Minnie and Moskowitz* (Gena Rowlands wins Best Actress New York Film Critics Circle Awards [2nd place] and Cassavetes is nominated for Best Comedy Screenplay by Writers Guild of America).

1972   Acts in *Columbo* episode with Peter Falk. First filmmaker-in-residence in the American Film Institute's Center for Advanced Film Studies and brings students in to work on *A Woman Under the Influence*.

1974   Writes and directs *A Woman Under the Influence*; presented at New York Film Festival. Garners fifteen national and international awards and nominations, including Academy Award nominations for Best Actress (Gena Rowlands) and Best Director (Cassavetes). Starts Faces International Film Company for distribution of his personal films.

1976   Stars in *Mikey and Nicky* (dir. Elaine May) with Peter Falk. Also writes and directs *The Killing of a Chinese Bookie*.

1977   Writes and directs *Opening Night* and distributes in Europe; Gena Rowlands wins Silver Bear for Best Actress at the 28th (1978) Berlin International Film Festival and Cassavetes is nominated for Golden

	Bear; Golden Globe nominations for Rowlands (Best Actress) and Joan Blondell (Best Supporting Actress).
1977–78	Acts in *The Fury* (dir. Brian de Palma) and *Brass Target* (dir. John Hough).
1980	Writes and directs *Gloria*; Gena Rowlands nominated for 1981 Best Actress Academy Award and Golden Globe Award; Cassavetes wins Golden Lion at 1980 Venice Film Festival.
1982	Stars in Paul Mazursky's *Tempest*.
1983	Receives medical prognosis of six months to live, though Cassavetes would live until 1989.
1984	Writes and directs *Love Streams*; wins Golden Bear Award at the 34th Berlin International Film Festival. Cassavetes considered this his "last film" because he hated his experience on the next film.
1986	Directs *Big Trouble*, a studio film taken over from Andrew Bergman who wrote screenplay; film re-edited against Cassavetes's wishes.
1987	Writes and stages three-act play *Woman of Mystery* in May–June at Court Theatre (Los Angeles) starring Gena Rowlands and Carol Kane.
1988	*Opening Night* premiered in the US at New York Film Festival as "New Film of the Year."
1989	Begins producing *She's Delovely* with Sean Penn but dies February 3 of cirrhosis of the liver at age fifty-nine, before resolving legal and financial problems. (In 1997, son Nick Cassavetes directed *She's So Lovely* from his father's screenplay, starring Sean Penn.) Buried in Westwood Village Memorial Park in Los Angeles.

Filmography

SHADOWS (1959)
Presented by Jean Shepherd's *Night People*
Producers: Maurice McEndree, Seymour Cassel (associate)
Director: **John Cassavetes**
Screenplay: **John Cassavetes**
Cinematography: Erich Kollmar
Production Design: Randy Liles, Bob Reeh
Editing: **John Cassavetes,** Maurice McEndree
Music: Shafi Hadi (saxophone solos); Charles Mingus (additional music)
Cast: Ben Carruthers (Ben), Lelia Goldoni (Lelia), Hugh Hurd (Hugh), Anthony Ray (Tony), Dennis Salas (Dennis), Tom Allen (Tom), David Pokitillow (David), Rupert Crosse (Rupert), Davey Jones (Davey), Pir Marini (Pir the Piano Player), Victoria Vargas (Vickie), Jack Ackerman (Jack, Director of Dance Studio), Jacqueline Walcott (Jacqueline), and others
16mm, b&w, 87 minutes (1957 version, 78 minutes)

TOO LATE BLUES (1961)
Producer: **John Cassavetes**
Director: **John Cassavetes**
Screenplay: **John Cassavetes,** Richard Carr
Cinematography: Lionel Lindon
Art Direction: Hal Pereira, Tambi Larsen
Costumes: Edith Head
Editing: Frank Bracht
Music: David Raksin
Cast: Bobby Darin (John "Ghost" Wakefield), Stella Stevens (Jess Polanski), Everett Chambers (Benny Flowers), Nick Dennis (Nick Bobolenos), Vince Edwards (Tommy Sheehan), Val Avery (Milt Frielobe), Marilyn Clark (Countess), James Joyce (Reno Vitelli), Rupert Crosse (Baby Jackson), Cliff Carnell (Charlie), Richard Chambers (Pete), Seymour Cassel (Red), Dan Stafford (Shelley), and others
35mm, color, 96 minutes

A CHILD IS WAITING (1962)
Distributed by United Artists
Producers: Stanley Kramer, Phillip Langner (associate)
Director: **John Cassavetes**
Screenplay: Abby Mann
Cinematography: Joseph LaShelle
Production Design: Rudolph Sternad
Costumes: Joe King (Judy Garland's wardrobe: Howard Shoup)
Editing: Gene Fowler Jr., Robert C. Jones
Music: Ernest Gold
Cast: Burt Lancaster (Dr. Matthew Clark), Judy Garland (Jean Hansen), Gena
Rowlands (Sophie Widdicombe Benham), Steven Hill (Ted Widdicombe), Paul
Stewart (Goodman), Gloria McGehee (Mattie), Lawrence Tierney (Douglas Ben-
ham), Bruce Ritchey (Reuben Widdicombe), John Marley (Holland), Bill Mumy
(Boy Counting Jean's Pearls), Elizabeth Wilson (Miss Fogarty), **John Cassa-
vetes** (Retarded adult walking toward camera—uncredited), and others
35mm, b&w, 102 minutes

FACES (1968)
Producers: **John Cassavetes** (uncredited), Maurice McEndree, Al Ruban
(associate)
Director: **John Cassavetes**
Screenplay: **John Cassavetes**
Cinematography: Al Ruban, Maurice McEndree (uncredited), Haskell Wexler
(uncredited)
Art Direction: Phedon Papamichael
Editing: Al Ruban, Maurice McEndree, **John Cassavetes** (uncredited)
Music: Jack Ackerman
Cast: John Marley (Richard Forst), Gena Rowlands (Jeannie Rapp), Lynn Carlin
(Maria Forst), Seymour Cassel (Chet), Fred Draper (Freddie Draper), Val Avery
(Jim McCarthy), Dorothy Gulliver (Florence), Joanne Moore Jordan (Louise
Draper), Darlene Conley (Billy Mae), Gene Darfler (Joe Jackson), Elizabeth
Deering (Stella), and others
35mm, color, 183 minutes

HUSBANDS (1970)
Distributed by Columbia Pictures
Producers: Al Ruban, Sam Shaw (associate)
Director: **John Cassavetes**
Screenplay: **John Cassavetes**

Cinematography: Victor Kemper
Art Direction: Rene D'Auriac
Costumes: Lewis Brown
Editing: Tom Cornwell, Robert Heffernan, Peter Tanner, Jack Woods
Music: Ray Brown
Cast: Peter Falk (Archie Black), Ben Gazzara (Harry), **John Cassavetes** (Gus Demetri), Jenny Runacre (Mary Tynan), Jenny Lee Wright (Pearl Billingham), Noelle Kao (Julie), Meta Shaw (Annie), Leola Harlow (Leola), Delores Delmar (The Countess), Eleanor Zee (Mrs. Hines), David Rowlands (Stuart Jackson), Judith Lowry (Grandmother), John Red Kullers (Red), and others
35mm, color, 138 minutes

MINNIE AND MOSKOWITZ (1971)
Distributed by Universal Pictures
Producers: Al Ruban, Paul Donnelly (associate)
Director: **John Cassavetes**
Screenplay: **John Cassavetes**
Cinematography: Michael Margulies, Alric Edens, Arthur J. Ornitz
Costumes: Helen Colvig
Editing: Fred Knudtson
Music: Bo Harwood
Cast: Gena Rowlands (Minnie Moore), Seymour Cassel (Seymour Moskowitz), Val Avery (Zelmo Swift), Tim Carey (Morgan Morgan), Katherine Cassavetes (Sheba Moskowitz), Elizabeth Deering (Girl), Elsie Ames (Florence), Lady Rowlands (Georgia Moore), Holly Near (Irish), Judith Roberts (Wife), Jack Danskin (Dick Henderson), Eleanor Zee (Mrs. Grass), Sean Joyce (Ned), David Rowlands (Minister), **John Cassavetes** (Jim, uncredited), and others
35mm, color, 114 minutes

A WOMAN UNDER THE INFLUENCE (1974)
Faces International Films, Distributed by Cine-Source
Producer: Sam Shaw
Director: **John Cassavetes**
Screenplay: **John Cassavetes**
Cinematography: Mitch Breit, Al Ruban
Art Direction: Phedon Papamichael
Costumes: Carole Smith
Editing: David Armstrong, Sheila Viseltear
Music: Bo Harwood
Cast: Gena Rowlands (Mabel Longhetti), Peter Falk (Nick Longhetti), Fred

Draper (George Mortensen), Lady Rowlands (Martha Mortensen), Katherine Cassavetes (Margaret Longhetti), Matthew Laborteaux (Angelo Longhetti), Matthew Cassel (Tony Longhetti), Christina Grisanti (Maria Longhetti), O. G. Dunn (Garson Cross), Mario Gallo (Harold Jensen), Eddie Shaw (Dr. Zepp), Angelo Grisanti (Vito Grimaldi), Charles Horvath (Eddie), James Joyce (Bowman), John Finnegan (Clancy), Vince Barbi (Gino), Cliff Carnell (Aldo), Frank Richards (Adolph), Hugh Hurd (Willie Johnson), Leon Wagner (Billy Tidrow), Dominique Davalos (Dominique Jensen), Xan Cassavetes (Adrienne Jensen), Pancho Meisenheimer (John Jensen), Sonny Aprile (Aldo), Ellen Davalos (Nancy), Joanne Moore Jordan (Muriel), Elizabeth Deering (Angela), Jackie Peters (Tina), Elsie Ames (Principal), N. J. Cassavetes (Adolph)
35mm, color, 155 minutes

THE KILLING OF A CHINESE BOOKIE (1976)
Faces Distribution
Producers: Al Ruban, Phil Burton (associate)
Director: **John Cassavetes**
Screenplay: **John Cassavetes**
Cinematography: Mitchell Breit, Al Ruban
Production Design: Phedon Papamichael
Editing: Tom Cornwell
Music: Bo Harwood
Cast: Ben Gazzara (Cosmo Vitelli), Timothy Agoglia Carey (Flo), Seymour Cassel (Mort Weil), Robert Phillips (Phil), Morgan Woodward (The Boss), John Red Kullers (The Accountant), Al Ruban (Marty Reitz), Azizi Johan (Rachel), Virginia Carrington (Mama), Meade Roberts (Mr. Sophistication), Alice Friedland (Sherry), Donna Marie Gordon (Margo Donnar), and others
35mm, color, 135 minutes

OPENING NIGHT (1977)
Castle Hill Productions, Faces Distribution
Producers: Al Ruban, Sam Shaw, Michael Lally (associate)
Director: **John Cassavetes**
Screenplay: **John Cassavetes**
Cinematography: Alan Ruban
Production Design: Bryan Ryman
Costumes: Alexandra Corwin-Hankin
Editing: Tom Cornwell
Music: Bo Harwood
Cast: Gena Rowlands (Myrtle Gordon), **John Cassavetes** (Maurice Aarons),

Ben Gazzara (Manny Victor), Joan Blondell (Sarah Goode), Paul Stewart (David Samuels), Zohra Lampert (Dorothy Victor), Laura Johnson (Nancy Stein), John Tuell (Gus Simmons), Ray Powers (Jimmy), John Finnegan (Propman), Louise Fitch (Kelly), Fred Draper (Leo), Katherine Cassavetes (Vivian), Lady Rowlands (Melva Drake), Carol Warren (Carla), Briana Carver (Lena), Angel Guisanti (Charlie Spikes), Meade Roberts (Eddie Stein), Eleanor Zee (Sylvia Stein), David Rowlands (Doorman), and others

35mm, color, 144 minutes

GLORIA (1980)
Distributed by Columbia Pictures
Producers: Sam Shaw, Stephen F. Kesten (associate)
Director: **John Cassavetes**
Screenplay: **John Cassavetes**
Cinematography: Fred Schuler
Art Direction: Rene D'Auriac
Costumes: Peggy Farrell and Emanuel Ungaro
Editing: George C. Villaseñor
Music: Bill Conti
Cast: Gena Rowlands (Gloria Swenson), Julie Carmen (Jeri Dawn), Tony Knesich (1st Man, Gangster), Gregory Cleghorne (Kid in Elevator), Buck Henry (Jack Dawn), John Adames (Phil Dawn), Lupe Garnica (Margarita Vargas), Jessica Castillo (Joan Dawn), Tom Noonan (2nd Man, Gangster), Ronald Maccone (3rd Man, Gangster), George Yudzevich (Heavy-Set Man), William E. Rice (TV Newscaster), and others

35mm, color, 123 minutes

LOVE STREAMS (1984)
Distributed by Cannon Films
Producers: Menachem Golan, Yoram Globus
Director: **John Cassavetes**
Screenplay: **John Cassavetes**, Ted Allan
Cinematography: Al Ruban
Editing: George C. Villaseñor
Music: Bo Harwood
Cast: Gena Rowlands (Sarah Lawson), **John Cassavetes** (Robert Harmon), Diahnne Abbott (Susan), Seymour Cassel (Jack Lawson), Margaret Abbott (Margarita), Jakob Shaw (Albie Swanson), Eddy Donno (Stepfather Swanson), Joan Foley (Judge Dunbar), Al Ruban (Milton Kravitz), Tom Badal (Sam the Lawyer),

Julie Allan (Charlene), Doe Avedon (Mrs. Kiner), Frank Beetson (Cashier), Neil
Bell (The Dog Man), Gregg Berger (Taxi Driver)
35mm, color, 141 minutes

BIG TROUBLE (1986)
Distributed by Columbia Pictures
Producer: Mike Lobell (uncredited)
Director: **John Cassavetes**
Screenplay: Andrew Bergman (as Warren Bogle)
Cinematography: Bill Butler
Production Design: Gene Callahan, Peter Landsdown Smith
Costumes: Joe I. Tompkins
Editing: Donn Cambern, Ralph E. Winters
Music: Bill Conti
Cast: Peter Falk (Steve Rickey), Alan Arkin (Leonard Huffman), Beverly D'Angelo
(Blanche Rickey), Charles Durning (O'Mara), Robert Stack (Winslow), Paul
Dooley (Noozel), Valerie Curtin (Arlene Hoffman), Richard Libertini (Dr. Lopez),
Steve Alterman (Peter Hoffman), Jerry Pavlon (Michael Hoffman), Paul LaGreca
(Joshua Hoffman), John Finnegan (Det. Murphy), Karl Lukas (Police Captain),
Maryedith Burrell (Gail), Edith Fields (Doris), and others
35mm, color, 93 minutes

John Cassavetes: Interviews

His'n and Her'n

Jesse Zunser / 1958

From *Cue*, June 7, 1958, 11, 14. Reprinted by permission of Sheila Zunser Rogoff.

The blonde gal from Wisconsin came to the Big City with stardust in her eyes and the guy from Queens crossed the bridge, and both dreamed of their names in lights, their pictures on billboards, and a zillion television screens bringing their faces (and talents) into the homes of all America.

"Well, now," said actor John Cassavetes the other day in the cozy living room of his Manhattan apartment, with lovely actress-wife Gena Rowlands looking on, "that wasn't *exactly* it. All I wanted was a job. I enrolled in the American Academy of Dramatic Arts—that's where I met Gena—and immediately thought I know all about acting. You know how it is with kids—you're scared you know nothing but sure you can play anything. I worked in Rhode Island stock a while and kicked around four years to land something. Then I got a job with Gregory Ratoff in a movie called *Taxi*."

That was something. "Ratoff couldn't pronounce my name so he called me 'The Greek.' He gave me two lines of dialogue and made me an assistant producer—in other words, messenger, valet, and office boy. From *Taxi* we moved into Broadway's *The Fifth Season* and the same set-up. When pressure got heavy Ratoff would yell he was losing his mind and he'd holler, 'The day that I am crazy I geev up fox hunting!' That was quite an experience and put me in a proper frame of mind to think of getting married. But first, of course, I had to quit my job—so I could be broke as well as a little crazy."

I looked at Gena (pronounced Jenna), imperturbably pouring coffee with queenly grace out of an exquisitely carved silver coffee set. She half-smiled like a blonde Mona Lisa, and said, "That's *his* story. He forgot to tell you I *had* a job, and a good one. I'd been on the road with *The Seven Year Itch* and came back to join the Broadway company. Before that, in Provincetown, because I knew one end of a needle from another, they made me wardrobe mistress. Then I toured with Melvyn Douglas in *Time Out for Ginger* and got in a year of television odds and ends." She looked at John. "He married a sound investment."

John eyed his investment appreciatively. "No complaints," he said.

Gena also left her job, and with the blessing of the Little Church Around the Corner and the high hopes of all newlyweds, the couple started hunting new jobs. Josh Logan hired Gena for the long-run Broadway hit *The Middle of the Night*, with Edward G. Robinson, a role that was to propel her to stardom and the movies. And John was signed for the bullfighter in TV's *Omnibus*'s "Paso Doble," *The Night Holds Terror*, *Crime in the Streets*, and ninety other television bits, big and small.

These brought him to Hollywood's attention and he was spotted into *Edge of the City* with Sidney Poitier, derived from the TV prizewinner *A Man Is Ten Feet Tall*, and *Saddle the Wind*, a walloping western with Robert Taylor.

Now, with a smartly decorated top-floor flat and penthouse on East 75th Street, with a postage-stamp-sized roof garden, with Central Park's greenery to the west and the whole great city that is their oyster all around, this drama-born couple—still newlywedding after four years—combine their private, public, and professional lives with ease.

Gena, whose mother was an artist, paints, sculpts, and plays the piano ("no Czerny and no Hanson, but plenty of Chopin—he takes a lot of practice"). John collects chess-sets ("some so old and fragile I'm afraid to play with them"), nails up bookshelves ("anybody can hammer a nail") and wonders, "Maybe I could get a couple of tons of earth up on this roof and raise our own vegetables—does one have weeds in a rooftop garden?" Besides making like a husband, house-holder, and farmer, John rents an office downtown "where I can work and be alone. Sometimes Gena and I work and rehearse with and against each other, but mostly, I think, it's good to work some things out by yourself."

In the movies, it seems, you never know what you're going to run into. Take westerns. "Great stuff," says John. "They get a city boy out into the open. In *Saddle the Wind* somebody spread a report I was the greatest rider alive. Why, I couldn't ride at all! They hoisted me aboard this four-legged package of muscled dynamite and I got thrown so fast I bounced before I hit. I got hoisted up again and got bounced again into the wild blue yonder. A third time up, and this time I grabbed that horse's mane and yelled, 'You four-legged so-and-so, I'm gonna ride you and you're gonna like it!' Well, I rode him sure enough, but the way that horse carried on I guess neither of us liked it. Maybe he figured like I did, well, it's a living."

The bell rang and Gena went to the door to get a package. She ran into the bed-room with it and came out a minute later wearing a blinding-red chemise dress whose shapeless, baggy, droopy lines hid the attractive curves of her body as completely as any burlap bag ever covered a bushel of potatoes.

John's mouth hung wide open. In all fairness it should be said that Gena did more for that dress than it ever did for her. "I adore them," she gurgled, "isn't it simply divine!" John grunted and Gena took that for approval.

"This ought to dispel the canard once and for all," he whispered, "that women dress for men. There's no man alive that wouldn't laugh his head off to see an otherwise pretty girl stumbling down the street in that silken potato sack." Gena looked at him coolly, and said, "No man knows anything about style."

"Nor about women, either," said John out of his long experience. "Best rule is, love 'em—don't try to understand 'em."

The Cassaveteses live and work in complete harmony. Gena has an MGM five-year, two-pictures-a-year contract, with freedom to do stage parts; and John "has a more flexible arrangement." Says Gena: "You know how people are—always oohing and aahing and I wonder how long *they'll* last, and all that. So we decided that whatever comes, wherever we go, we go together. So many things happen in separation. And for us it has worked out fine—on Broadway, in Hollywood, to the Caribbean shooting pictures, the Virgin Islands, Italy, France, Switzerland, England. Even New York."

"When Gena is working," says John, "like for *The High Cost of Loving*, I didn't mind being out there in Hollywood with her. Doing nothing while she's busy doesn't give me any feeling of frustration because she's busy and I'm not. Sometimes it's the other way around. I'm working—or we're both busy."

And Gena: "When John's working I have a wonderful time. So many things to do, so many places to go, so many new things to learn, to see, to buy."

As a sort of peace offering to their good fortune John helped start an acting class at Burt Lane's Drama Workshop ("I think it's the best school in town"), and got involved in an amateur movie-making project—a picture that will never be shown commercially, "because nobody knows who owns it. We started it," says John, "as a school project, but had no money. Then one night I mentioned it on Jean Shepherd's *Night People* radio program, and the next day dollar bills began rolling in.

"We finished the picture and can't sell it because everybody worked for nothing and we can never trace all the people who sent in money to help make it. But it will be shown in a couple of festivals, including the Venice."

The critics have generally been good to the Cassaveteses, "but they do sometimes baffle us. Can a critic, for example, tell the difference between a bad script and bad direction, a bad performance or bad cutting? I sometimes wonder.

"One Hollywood reporter wrote that I 'acted like a guy who came out West with a New Yorkese accent.' Now, what does that mean? Maybe the author should have made me come from a Bronx finishing school."

Most actors have enough ego even after a critical blast to carry them over the rough criticism hurdles. "But what about the poor authors, the guys who write with blood and sweat and tears, and maybe if this play isn't good their next may be," said John. "What happens to them when the critics get out their long knives for a carving-up job?"

One of our best playwrights, a television writer with a long record of prizewinners, "is terrified of doing a Broadway play. The critics have him scared. Half a dozen men sitting in judgment—maybe tired, bored, dyspeptic, maybe not. But does a writer get a chance in today's theatre to test his work on the public? He can never even bring his case to the jury—the judges decide before the jury hears a word."

Cassavetes wants to be a director. He's made a picture in the Virgin Islands, soon to be released—the drama of a sheriff who persecutes a suspect and finally hounds him to death. "The moral," says John, "is: In trying to destroy others, we destroy ourselves. I play it with Sidney Poitier, and that guy makes any picture a great picture. . . ."

"John is good, too," said Gena. "*She's* not bad either," said John.

What's Wrong with Hollywood

John Cassavetes / 1959

From *Film Culture*, April 15, 1959, 4–5. Provided courtesy of Anthology Film Archives, All Rights Reserved.

Hollywood is not failing. It has failed. The desperation, the criticisms, the foolish solutions, the wholesale cutting of studio staffs and salaries, the various new technical improvements, the "bigger picture," and the "ultra-low-budget picture," have failed to put a stop to the decline.

The fact is that filmmaking, although unquestionably predicated on profit and loss like any other industry, cannot survive without individual expression. Motion pictures can not be made to please solely the producer's image of the public. For, as has been proved, this pleasure results neither in economic nor artistic success.

On the other hand, the audience itself, other-directed and mass-minded as it is, may condemn pictures such as *Twelve Angry Men* or *The Goddess*. These pictures may lose money, but they have inspired applause from those who still think freely and for themselves. These pictures have gone beyond Hollywood "formulas" and "ingredients," and will affect strongly the future of American motion pictures.

More often than not, the mass audience will not accept a new idea, an unfamiliar emotion, or a different point of view if it is presented in one or two films only, just as it will not immediately accept new ideas in life. However, the new thoughts must eventually lead to change.

This is not to say that individual expression need only be so-called point-of-view films or films that stimulate thought. Certainly the standard of the musical can and must be improved too; the treatment of comedy should reach in other directions; the "epic" and "Western" pictures and the "love story" must also search for more imaginative approaches and fresher ideas.

However, the probability of a resurrection of the industry through individual expression is slim, for the men of new ideas will not compromise themselves to Hollywood's departmental heads. These artists have come to realize that to compromise an idea is to soften it, to make an excuse for it, to betray it.

In Hollywood the producer intimidates the artist's new thought with great sums of money and with his own ego that clings to past references of box office triumphs and valueless experience. The average artist, therefore, is forced to compromise. And the cost of the compromise is the betrayal of his basic beliefs. And so the artist is thrown out of motion pictures, and the businessman makes his entrance.

However, in no other activity can a man express himself as fully as in art. And, in all times, the artist has been honored and paid for revealing his opinion of life. The artist is an irreplaceable figure in our society too: A man who can speak his own mind, who can reveal and educate, who can stimulate or appease, and in every sense communicate with fellow human beings. To have this privilege of world-wide communication in a world so incapable of understanding, and ignore its possibilities, and accept a compromise—most certainly will and should lead the artist and his films to oblivion.

Without individual creative expression, we are left with a medium of irrelevant fantasies that can add nothing but slim diversion to an already diversified world. The answer cannot be left in the hands of the money men, for their desire to accumulate material success is probably the reason they entered into filmmaking in the first place. The answer must come from the artist himself. He must become aware that the fault is his own: that art and the respect due his vocation as an artist is his own responsibility. He must, therefore, make the producer realize, by whatever means at his disposal, that only by allowing the artist full and free creative expression will the art and the business of motion pictures survive.

The Chip's Off His Shoulder

TV Guide / 1959

From *TV Guide*, November 28, 1959. Reprinted by permission of *TV Guide*.

John Cassavetes has undergone a metamorphosis since his most recent visit to Hollywood. The lean, intense young New Yorker has learned to love the hated Hollywood. (All New York actors, as all Hollywood actors will tell you, hate Hollywood.)

"When I was offered the *Staccato* series, I liked it," said Cassavetes, by way of introduction. "I liked the character and I thought we could do something really creative with this show. In my mind, there is no question about *if* it will be a success. It's *going* to be a success. If it isn't, then people don't like what I think they like, and I'll leave the business."

There had been talk that Cassavetes would use predominantly New York actors in the NBC series.

"We're using good actors," he said quickly, "and good actors can be found both here and in New York. We have Eduardo Ciannelli as a regular. He's a Hollywood actor from way back, and go find me a better one."

Some of *Staccato* has been filmed on location in New York, the hero's fictional base of operations. In fact, there was one night's work in Manhattan that must have made Hollywood look like heaven to Cassavetes.

He and a crew from the West Coast were shooting exterior scenes for future shows. In eight hours they filmed their way from the Polo Grounds to tenement doorways in Harlem and the Lower East Side, from fashionable Fifth Avenue to a Bowery mission.

En route, the star almost was hit by a falling crate of books; was doused with a pitcher of water by a citizen who didn't like the Hollywood-style commotion; and for an hour dashed back and forth across Fifth Avenue, dodging taxicabs and buses. By the dawn's early light, the lean Cassavetes was several pounds leaner.

"I came to Hollywood with a lot of preconceived notions," he continued. "When New Yorkers came back from California, they were always so terribly happy to be back. They claimed their creative prowess had been stopped. They complained about the 'powers that be.' So I was prepared to fight on sight.

"Things weren't very pleasant at first. People in Hollywood seemed to have pretty much the same preconceived notions about New Yorkers that we had about them. There was an air of unspoken condescension and quiet hostility. There was a great deal of tension between me and the producer, the network people and the agency people. Each of us expected the other to be 'different,' so our defense mechanisms were cocked.

"Well, I've finally discovered that the 'they' my New York friends were always complaining about really didn't exist except in the mind. I went through a long soul-searching bit one night, and when I got to the set the next morning I found that the whole attitude had somehow changed. The production manager came up to me and said, 'John—anything you want, you ask for. Just ask nicely, and you'll get it. Just be reasonable, that's all.'

"Anyway, as of right now I have never worked harder or been happier.

"I said in the beginning that there was no question about *if* this show will be a success, that it was *going* to be a success. Well, I still feel that. We've had a rough start and some pretty rough reviews. You guys at *TV Guide* [Oct. 24] were as rough on us as anyone, but I'm not mad. It just hurts when I bleed.

"We've needed time to get rolling, time to find the best writers and directors. If you put a 100-percent effort into something, and you have succeeded before by giving out with that 100-percent effort, then it's going to work," Cassavetes concluded. "I don't just *feel* that—I *know* it."

Mr. John Cassavetes on the Actor and Improvisation

Our Special Correspondent / 1960

From the *Times* (London), August 11, 1960. Reprinted by permission of News Syndication (London).

Mr. John Cassavetes, who was in London last week to discuss his film projects, is a young actor with firm and individual ideas on his craft and on the art of filmmaking. They are ideas which command all the more respect since they were attested by Mr. Cassavetes's own first feature film as a director, *Shadows*, which was reviewed in the *Times* on its first showing at the National Film Theatre, and is shortly due for commercial release in London.

Mr. Cassavetes is thirty, and looks, perhaps, younger—even boyish. He talks about his work enthusiastically and fluently, in spite of constant protestations that he is "inarticulate." He began his career as an actor in a stock company, then went to Broadway as assistant stage manager of *The Fifth Season*. In recent years, however, he has worked mostly in the cinema and television. In this country he is best known for his playing in *A Man Is Ten Feet Tall* and *Crime in the Streets*, and in the television series *Johnny Staccato*, several episodes of which he directed himself.

His first chance to experiment on independent lines came when he established an actors' workshop in New York—the Variety Arts Studio. He gathered together a group of talented young unknown actors; and it was here that they first worked out the improvisations which led to *Shadows*. The history of the film is already well known. One of the improvisations was filmed. Shown on television, it was received with such enthusiasm that the team was encouraged to build improvisation on improvisation, until—after laborious editing sessions by Mr. Cassavetes and his editor, Len Apelson—they had completed a feature-length film.

Mr. Cassavetes is convinced of the pre-eminence of the actor, whether in cinema or theatre. *Shadows* had no script; the director's role was primarily to coordinate the work. The real creators were the actors themselves; and for Mr.

Cassavetes this is an ideal way of creation. He takes a special view of the role of the ensemble. "If the film is primarily the creation of the director or the writer, then you have only a single viewpoint upon the theme. It is the creation of only one imagination. But if the film is created out of the actors, then the work has as many facets as there are actors; the action is seen in the round—the communal creation of several imaginations."

Within this framework the creative role of each individual actor is of prime importance. Mr. Cassavetes—diverging from the working method advocated by Stanislavsky and followed, notably, by the Actors Studio—is opposed to group discussion of the characters. Each role must, he feels, be an individual's conception as well as an individual creation. Only like this, he says, can you achieve a genuine collision in the relationships between characters. If each role is the result of communal study by director and ensemble, "everything will dovetail; it will all be nice and neat and smooth; but the conflict of the characters won't be truthful."

Shadows provides a practical demonstration. The relationships established there are recognizably more real than we are accustomed to in the majority of scripted films. As they talk, the characters' words and reactions betray suspicions and fears and affections, intuitions and incomprehensions, with a subtlety generally beyond the means of normal screen method.

Does this mean that Mr. Cassavetes sees as an ideal a purely improvisational theatre and cinema? Acknowledging the obvious thematic limitations of the method, he feels that it is capable of fairly wide application. Can his system be applied to literary drama? "Certainly. First we improvise to get the feel of the characters; then as the actors become easy in the roles we go back to the text. If it doesn't work out, then we go back and improvise some more; and again return to the text. We keep working like this till we feel complete identification between actor and role."

Again, however, Mr. Cassavetes is opposed to the Stanislavsky system of minute textual discussion. "The general theme of the work, of course, must be studied by the whole group, so that we share the same overall conceptions but each actor must come at his own interpretation of his role, without the sort of group study and mutual criticism which one associates with Method work."

Clearly the severest limitation of Mr. Cassavetes's ideal of the actor's theatre is the ability of the actors. As an actor, Mr. Cassavetes has great faith in his colleagues, "as long as they are given praise. That's what an actor needs. Praise is his prime nourishment." Each actor must discover his own working method. "That was Stanislavsky's real idea. He offered some concrete indications, of course; but he acknowledged that every artist must in the end discover his own, personal method." For Mr. Cassavetes the free improvisation is the best means of discovering this personal method. *Shadows* argues well for him.

Cassavetes and Pogostin in "Artistic" Clash with Universal

Dave Kaufman / 1966

For as long as there has been Hollywood, there has been a bitter rivalry between those who are creative, and those who represent the business interests. Clashes are inevitable, although the crescendo of this rivalry has dimmed in recent years, particularly in TV where creators have less and less to say about the final work. And so it was behind-the-scenes on "Face of Change," a "Bob Hope–Chrysler Theatre" segment which airs on NBC-TV December 28, a time of the year when viewing is normally down, as people leave their sets for holidaying.

John Cassavetes, Diane Baker, Ben Gazzara, Suzy Parker, and a newcomer, John Silver, appear in this drama, written and directed for Universal TV by S. Lee Pogostin. When Cassavetes saw the script he was so enthused he offered to work for scale. His offer was gladly accepted, and it can be assumed did not offend those on the business end of the operation.

Why did he pass up his usual price to toil for scale? "I thought it was important to do it on this show, to make a statement. The money is not important," replies Cassavetes, and Pogostin adds, "John would normally get the top price on the show." Since he did this, the actor has passed up $37,000 in various offers because he didn't care for the scripts, and, he admits, "I could use the money."

But troubles were ahead for both on "Change," which Pogostin describes as "the story of a man who passionately loves LA. He says she's got lots of shapes, but has no shape. He's a jazz musician, he goes out in the streets and says you don't need LSD if you use your senses, but nobody is listening."

Cassavetes: "He's a musician, and they don't listen anymore to anything. What this show says is that there is something important in people, something they possess that's become so cynical that it's dying—the senses, a universal thing. We can't agree on politics, but maybe we can agree on senses."

Pogostin: "We forget to use our senses, 90 percent of them aren't used. If you go to the gut of it, you realize you're using only a small fraction of what's been given us."

Cassavetes: "Nobody has any time anymore, nobody has time to listen. In our story, people think I'm a nut because I try to awaken their senses. My orchestra, my friends and me—we are ready to attempt mass suicide, to jump off a building, to arouse everybody."

But problems developed during the production, and Cassavetes says of Universal: "They threatened me with a suit, they said I was difficult." Why? "Universal follows the pattern, the budget. They are bankers, we are creative, but they object to that. We don't object to their being bankers. They consider me difficult. The story is original, and it makes them nervous. Making people think is dangerous, it's better to imitate, they think."

Pogostin: "We went over one day, but not on budget . . . Having tried to say what I needed to say, I said it, and now they're burying us on December 28."

Cassavetes takes the view that "90 percent of the producers aren't necessary. They're only in the way of the production department and everyone else . . . Only in LA is artist a dirty word. Arty is about the worst thing you can say here . . . We are dying of sadness. The whole world is dying of sadness. We are the enemy. I'm afraid to say the bankers have no talent, and they have none. We are the whores—not them. They never sell out. They have killed creative talent."

While Pogostin is in agreement with Cassavetes regarding the "Change" show, they disagree as regards the broader picture of a studio nullifying creativeness. Pogostin feels the actor is too rough on Universal in this respect, pointing out they let him work on his properties with a fairly free hand. But Cassavetes seems to feel Pogostin's phrase, "they let me," is beneath him, and there is a sharp dispute on this point. Which ends with Pogostin retorting if he finds there is interference with his work, "I can always go back to my island off Spain."

Masks and Faces: John Cassavetes in an Interview with David Austen

David Austen / 1968

From *Films and Filming* (London), September 1968, 4–6, 8.

John Cassavetes: My roots are in America. There's really no section of society there that I'm not in some way aware of, mostly through travelling around the country. I lived in New York a great deal of my life and spent quite a while in repertories and stock touring throughout about thirteen or fourteen states. I've been down South and in the Midwest and in the Chicago area, and, of course, I've commuted back and forth between the East and the West coasts. So I know a little bit about the way people think in their different areas and walks of life. I know what their humor is and what their tolerance levels are and something about what they're looking for. The problem with the people in America is that they are so politically orientated, so economically orientated, that they keep what they really feel, their private thoughts, quite to themselves. Maybe they do share it with their families, but they do it as a secret. They've got their own kind of underground working for them—I know this. I know if I come to England, and I've spent a great deal of time here now over the past ten years, I mean, I just don't know anything about it.

David Austen: Did you get any offers, from home or abroad, to direct films after *Shadows*?

JC: No . . . none at all, I'm a director, but I do like to make films. Making films means having an idea that you have to talk about and not knowing what it is that's disturbing you, so that it's an adventure all the way. What's basically wrong with Hollywood is that you cannot really have team-work on a commercial film. I couldn't make a good film without it. There is a compromise made if you work on a commercial film and the compromise really isn't how or what you do, the techniques you use, or even the content, but really the compromise is beginning to feel a lack of confidence in your innermost thoughts. And if you don't put these innermost thoughts on the screen then you are looking down on not only your audience but the people you work with, and that's what makes so many people working out there unhappy. They say: "Well, I'll make a lot of money and then I'll come back and do this later on," and the truth of the matter is, of course, that they never do. These innermost thoughts become less and less a part of you and once you lose them then you don't have anything else. I don't think anyone does it purposely, it's just that a lot of people are not aware of losing these things.

I found myself losing them too, and then suddenly I woke up and by accident, by sheer accident of not getting along with something, something inside, you know, you say: "No, I must struggle with this thing . . ." without any knowledge of what it is making you do this. You fight and consequently you don't work and when you don't work you go back and reevaluate yourself, reevaluate your life, your relationship to the world or whatever it is that's important to you. In that period of time I gathered a great deal of food, not energy any more out of my youth, not a feeling of wanting to conquer anything, not "Yes, it can be done, let's do it, what's the problem?" but a feeling of saying that so many people have so much to say and there are so many really worthwhile things to say that it seems impossible that we could cut ourselves off from this whole avenue of enormous excitement.

DA: After *Shadows* you were very often quoted as saying you would like to give up acting and concentrate on directing. Was this subject to reevaluation?
JC: I am inconsistent . . . well, a filmmaker has to be crazy. Ideas run rampant, you know. I reckon I've ten pictures I'd like to make and the reason for it is that the people that you want to work with have opened themselves up so much . . . it's like discovering some kind of well that's untapped and there's no way to get at it because there's not enough time to do it and you don't want to tell anyone about it . . . so you get greedy, you just want to hold on to these things . . .

DA: What about the projects you have worked on? Right now we're waiting for *Rosemary's Baby*.
JC: I think it's a very good picture. It's all been very well done, the photography and sets are magnificent.

DA: There were some difficulties . . .
JC: I guess there was a conflict of personalities. Polanski and I just don't like each other, but I think he's a fine director and I'd work for him any time.

DA: Then there was *The Devil's Angels*.

JC: Dan Haller, the director, is a very sweet guy. He's very artistic and very honest, and he came to me and said, "Look, this thing is really an exploitive movie, but I'd really like to try to accomplish something within that framework." And so I figured that I'd learn to ride a motorcycle, be with some people out on location and just open up a little more. Within its given area Dan did a very good job with it.

DA: And *The Dirty Dozen*?

JC: I loved working with Aldrich. From an actor's point of view, he and Siegel are my two favorites. It's very simple to work for them because they deal with you as you would treat a friend who you respect and who you could talk to . . . they're fine people.

DA: How did *Faces* come about?

JC: I've always been around with a great many people who are very creative. As I see it you can't be creative at an early age without having them around you. You really do need somebody to talk to because ideas have to formulate before you put them into action. They have to come out of good times, they have to come out of comfort. You can't go around being on your guard all your life and talk about some kind of freedom, so we all make it a point to find each other, to be friends, to share each other's needs and ideas, to talk about people honestly and never to lie to each other. I was working in a commercial area trying to figure out what to do. I didn't have an idea. I hadn't had an idea since *A Child Is Waiting*, because there wasn't anything happening in the world that I could relate to, there didn't seem to be any specific problem or subject that I was concerned with at that time.

DA: There was some trouble with *A Child Is Waiting*.

JC: It was strictly a commercial venture. From my point of view it was a painful experience, not because of the retarded children, but from the fact that it's really hard to compromise a subject that shouldn't be compromised. It's in the past now anyway. Somehow you survive these disappointments and go on working.

I never felt I could write anything, and after *A Child Is Waiting* I was relegated to obscurity both as an actor and as a director. So I sat at home and wrote. I wrote anything I felt like. I must have written fifty half-scripts. I read newspapers and books and so on. Then one day the producer Maurice McEndree said, "Why don't we do something?" and I said, "Well, there's a lot of things I've written at home and I'm sure we can find something that will be interesting to do." I had written something on a plane—it was about ten pages of some dialogue between two men who were talking about what it used to be like in the old days. We thought it would be the best thing to do because it was about marriage, middle age, and the society we live in. We were in California, so we thought we might as well do it there. I sat down and wrote about three weeks' worth of script. It came to 206 pages, and then it was only half completed.

DA: Was this in story form or a dialogue script?
JC: It was a stream of consciousness, just anything that came into my mind. The script was never edited. We had decided to do it and so we just had to start shooting. We had an office at Screen Gems at that time and John Marley, who plays Richard Frost in the film, came over. He picked it up and read it and said, "Gee, what a heck of a good part! Can I play it?" And I said, "Sure! We'll make it as a play. We're going to do it as a play." So John asked to be counted in. And so people kept coming up and as they did they saw the script and they read it and so we gradually cast the picture.

That was October, 1964. We started shooting the film on January 1, 1965.

DA: Were the conditions for making *Faces* very much the same as for *Shadows*?
JC: No, they weren't. They were quite different really.

Shadows was an experiment. It predominantly came out of a workshop. We were improvising on a story, one that was in my mind. It was my secret. Every scene in *Shadows* was very simple; they were predicated on people having problems that were overcome with other problems; at the end of a scene another problem would come in and overlap. This carried it forward and built up a simple structure. Once I had the structure it was a matter of writing a character breakdown and then working on that with the individual. There was a struggle because firstly I had never done a film before, and secondly the actors had to find the confidence to have quiet at times, and not just constantly talk. This took about the first three weeks of the schedule. Eventually all this material was thrown away, and then everyone became cool and easy and relaxed and they had their own things to say, which was the point.

When we started to work on *Faces* there was a combination of professional and amateur actors. And the subject was one which I knew absolutely nothing about, even though I'm married and live in a rich middle-class strata of society. It was something I've been aware of, but at the same time didn't understand; so I was compelled to take people that I felt could add something and understand something of the subject that we were dealing with. It would be a mutual discovery, and from my point of view it was simply a question of stimulating an honest appraisal on each person's part of what their life would be, and the minute we got that straightened out then the shooting became quite easy.

It took five months. We were finished on June 1, 1965. We shot nearly every day. Sometimes we would take a couple of weeks off, you know, to think about a scene, and then come back when we got too deep in it, or we became too involved with each other on a personal level, or were getting too pleased with the work, then we came back and started refreshed.

I'm the sole financier but I'm not too sure of the final cost. I believe it's in the vicinity of $200,000 . . . and that was on 16mm.

DA: Weren't there one or two shots on 35mm . . . in the "morning after" sequence, for example?

JC: No, that was on Plus X Reversal. We were using different stock on every scene. For instance, where they all come into Jeannie's apartment, the lighting man said, "Look, it's five o'clock in the afternoon, and it's always grainy to me. Do you mind if I shoot it that way?" So he lit it purposely that way to get the grainy feeling of that time in the afternoon, when you've got a few drinks in you. The morning after should be crisp and kind of light and beautiful, so he used a different stock. We shot on Tri X Reversal for the nightclub scenes. And on the final sequences in the house we had to get a very natural feeling, so we used Double X and available light. At night in the living room we had to use Four X because . . . well, I'm a maniac: I shoot for the actors and not the technicians. Nobody was marked, and it wasn't a question of whether or not the operator wanted to use a hand-held camera . . . he just didn't have the time to set up; the actors were starting and he had to get rolling.

DA: How much direction do you give for camera movement?

JC: I rarely look through the camera, so the operator really has to get on with it. I say, "This is what I'm after . . . what do you think?" So he has an opportunity to fulfill himself creatively and have total responsibility. At times he would say, "Look, I don't have a feeling for this . . ." and somebody else would take that shot . . . either I would shoot it, or Al Ruban, or the producer.

DA: The first cut was just under four hours.

JC: About that. But after the initial screening we made some cuts and got it down to three hours, three minutes. We weren't sure about taking that version to Montreal, but we did, and it was gratifying. There was a tremendous vocal response from that audience. But it is a long time to sit there and be emotionally involved . . . you get tired, it drains you. Now we've cut it down to two hours, ten minutes, and this was the version we showed here at the National Film Theatre. Every sequence was shortened and the McCarthy scene was cut considerably; it was originally an hour and twenty minutes long, and that's a movie in itself. Nobody became involved in *Faces* for any financial return, so it wasn't important that the film had to be palatable . . . in the sense of pleasing.

You can see a film with an audience and half of them may like it and the rest walk out. The second screening you have 15 percent of your audience walk out. The next one only 10 percent of them get up and leave. And finally, you make all the adjustments and none of the audience walks out. Everybody likes it. And all of a sudden you find yourself hating the film. That can happen.

I haven't seen *Shadows* since the day we finished it. It's really a brutal thing, but I have no further interest once a picture has been finalized. I don't think I will ever see *Faces* again. It's like a love affair that's gone.

DA: What of future projects?

JC: I have to go to Rome to make a picture. I'm acting in that one . . . with Peter Falk, Britt Ekland, Gena Rowlands, and Edward G. Robinson. It's a melodrama, quite interesting, and they're good parts.

Then I'm making one with Peter Falk and Ben Gazzara. We found a subject that we like: "Whatever Happened to Sentiment in the World Today?" So we're going to do a picture on Sentiment . . . I think the idea's exciting. Originally we didn't want a director on it at all, but the people who are putting up the money want the assurance of a director being on the project. So I'll direct it, still on the understanding that it's a cooperative venture. I'm doing the first draft script—it's called *The Husbands*.

I have maybe three more films to make and then I'm going to start to raise $5 million to go into a film repertory company. To me the actors are the most important thing in the world . . . they are the instruments of interpretation. There will always be people who will sit down and write stories, and there will always be people who will want to direct them, to make them into films, but it becomes increasingly more difficult to find people to interpret those films, because there is so little value or respect given to those people. It isn't the typewritten word that you see up there, it's people . . . and if they don't interpret with some human feeling that the audience can relate to . . . well, I think that films will be in trouble eventually. So I want to set this project up that will be dedicated to the actor's performance. It will have to be for a two-year period; after that it would just become the same. It will be a time for reevaluation. Movies are getting to be too much the same.

Man of Many Shattered Faces

Deac Rossell / 1968

From *Boston After Dark*, December 18, 1968. Reprinted by permission of Deac Rossell.

John Cassavetes lives in two worlds. Not only is he an actor (from TV's drama days to *Rosemary's Baby*) and a director (from *Shadows*, 1960, to *Faces*, 1968), but his work in both fields also covers a spectrum from entertainment extravaganzas marketed through regular channels to independent films that have initiated new styles of personal, honest filmmaking and distribution.

It is important to separate Cassavetes's dual career from the current fad of actor-directors in the commercial filmmaking community. This season, it is fashionable for American actors and even actresses to begin to direct films. Ingrid Bergman has just announced that she will direct a film in Europe next year, and veteran Katharine Hepburn has already set plans for her first directorial effort. Paul Newman's first picture *Rachel, Rachel* has been seen across the country. Alan Arkin, who has completed two short films, told me recently that he would like to direct features.

Step right up, folks! Who's next? Barbra Streisand? Sean Connery? Anybody got—or want—a camera? So far, on this reporter's scorecard, the 1968–69 flurry looks about as important to the film world as the forgotten efforts of such actors-flirting-with-direction as Ray Milland (*A Man Alone*, 1954; *Lisbon*, 1956), Burt Lancaster (*The Kentuckian*, 1955), and James Cagney (*Short Cut to Hell*, 1958).

Cassavetes is another case entirely. After much acting for television, including a starring part in the series *Johnny Staccato*, he produced his first independent film, *Shadows* (1960). The improvised story of a love affair between a white youth and a black girl, *Shadows* had a major impact on the film community, much like the initial romance of actor-director Orson Welles with Hollywood after *Citizen Kane*. Cassavetes was signed, like Welles, to a multi-picture contract with Paramount, to produce a series of low-budget art films. When the first film, *Too Late Blues* (1961) with Bobby Darin and Stella Stevens, was finished and declared a commercial failure, the project was shelved and Cassavetes was back on the street.

Yet his efforts were not totally in vain. Paul Leutrat, in his book on the "New

American Cinema" (*Jeune Cinema Americain*, Premier Plan No. 46), states flatly that "Before *Shadows*, independent American cinema virtually did not exist. After *Shadows* it became a reality." Cassavetes himself gives credit for starting the independent revolution to a man forgotten in his own time, Lionel Rogosin, who made *On the Bowery* in New York in 1956, but there is little doubt that *Shadows* was the right film at the right moment to encourage a whole series of New York filmmakers, from Shirley Clarke and the Mekas brothers right down to John Korty and Robert Downey.

But, apparently, *Too Late Blues* was the wrong film at the wrong time. The following year, 1962, Cassavetes made *A Child Is Waiting*, about emotionally disturbed and retarded children (with Burt Lancaster and Judy Garland). Nothing happened. So, after six years and featured roles in *The Dirty Dozen* and *Rosemary's Baby*, he wrote and directed *Faces*, which has led to a ride on a horse of a different color on the directing merry-go-round.

Faces won six international prizes at the Venice Film Festival this year, including a Best Actor award for John Marley. The film was shot over a period of six months, with a cast of professional and amateur actors, and then lingered in its can for two-and-a-half years, while editing and retakes were made on weekends snatched between other commitments.

"*Faces* is not a controversial picture in any sense of the word," Cassavetes said, last week in a Sheraton Plaza luncheon interview. "It is not about politics, the generation gap, sex, or anything like that. Yet people walk out of the theatre after seeing *Faces* and say the film was painful." If so, it is the pain of honesty, of seeing characters on the screen involved in exactly the kind of self-deception many people practice daily and don't like to admit.

"I'm a part of these people," Cassavetes said. "They do things I have done, or I have thought of, if I haven't done them myself. Today, we accept cheapness very lightly. People don't stand up for the important things in life, and soon, the unimportant things assume a major function, and that's all we are left with."

Cassavetes remarked that when he talks to people about *Faces* the conversation inevitably turns to a discussion of the kind of people he has pictured on the screen, their problems, and the ways they relate to the mainstream of American society instead of the usual questions about "How did you make the film?" and "What happened on the set?" Certainly the film is one of the few motion pictures where the content—what is being said and acted on the screen—is more important than a mechanical plot where we ask "Who did it?"

The way Cassavetes went about making the film has had a lot to do with its success in portraying realistic people. "I don't think that writing in film today is very good—but that doesn't matter much, because good writing does not guarantee a good film. I think it is the concept of the film that is important—our film failed when it didn't tell you anything."

The director went on to say that he functioned more like a "general manager" than as a director during the shooting of *Faces*: "I wrote it, but the actors interpreted it. I can't have the cumulative experience of all those people on the screen; it would be impossible for me. So I chose people to act in the film who were willing to reveal something about themselves as people in front of the camera.

"The ideas for my films start mostly with myself," Cassavetes continued. "I have to talk about my next film, *Husbands*; I can't talk about *Faces* any more. In *Husbands*, the idea is about a person of sentiment. Every scene in the picture will be our opinions about sentiment. I try to talk to the actors and try to find out what I really think about sentiment. It may turn harsh, or bitter; but I can allow anything as long as I know we are honest."

Cassavetes's honesty allows him to make all kinds of pictures. He asserted that he liked *The Dirty Dozen*, and enjoys acting in entertainment movies. "I'm glad not everyone is making this type of film, like *Faces*," he said, "or else I wouldn't go to movie theatres any more. I've often said that I don't feel like going to see an art picture—and I make them!"

He does not want to give up either of his two careers ("I'd hate like hell if actors weren't important."), or either of his two worlds. To him, acting is the "ultimate expression," simplified to the point where it is the actor against the world. "It's a personal contest, like the feeling a bullfighter must have," he asserted. "You have all your roots and deficiencies and insufficiencies showing."

There are few insufficiencies in *Faces*. John Cassavetes turned all his energies toward structuring a film about real people caught in a real situation: two people who love each other, who are faced with a minor crisis, the results of which are blown out of all proportion—as he sees it.

"Filmmakers by nature don't have any causes," he stated bluntly, "they simply have subjects. A filmmaker is a cold man, really. The only excitement I could see in the film is a continuity of life in the actor's expression. I try to make people be as real as they can, to make them as natural as they can be."

The Director/Actor:
A Talk with John Cassavetes

Russell AuWerter / 1970

From *Action* 5(1) (January–February 1970). Permission to reprint courtesy of the Directors Guild of America, Inc.

John Cassavetes recently completed *Husbands*, his fifth film as director. In three of his films, *Shadows*, *Faces*, and *Husbands*, he has had complete artistic control from story selection through promotion. He wrote the screenplays for his two most recent films, *Faces* and *Husbands*. In *Husbands*, the story of three middle-aged, middle-class Americans on a spree in London, Cassavetes stars along with Ben Gazzara and Peter Falk. Cassavetes's highly personal style of direction resulted in his first film, *Shadows*, winning the Critics Award at the Venice Film Festival. *Faces* won five awards at the Venice Film Festival and received three Academy Award nominations. Cassavetes has acted in ninety television dramas, including his own series *Staccato*, and has acted in ten feature films—winning high critical praise for his role of the husband in *Rosemary's Baby* and an Oscar nomination for his role in *The Dirty Dozen*.

Born in New York of Greek immigrant parents, Cassavetes attended Colgate University and the American Academy of Dramatic Arts. He now lives in Los Angeles with his wife, the actress Gena Rowlands, and his two children. He was interviewed by Russell AuWerter, who writes on film topics for many publications.

AuWerter: What were the circumstances of your decision to become a director?

Cassavetes: I never really decided to become a director. I had a lot of very talented actor friends who were out of work in New York. I was working and actors help each other. You can't recommend an actor to a director or a producer or a writer—they have to discover for themselves what kind of an actor he is. So we got together and thought we would open a workshop. I found a space on West 48th Street—the old Malin Studios. It wasn't to be a school. It was to be a place where people could just perform and I could invite all the casting people down to see these actors perform. Well, as it turned out, the actors were offended by this and no one showed up. I had rented the place for a year at quite a bit of money, so I thought I'd better take an ad in the paper. I took ads in *Show Business*, in the *New York Times*, *Daily News*, and *Mirror*. People started coming in. Many, many people came in—from all walks of life—all wanting to be actors. I wasn't a teacher or a director—had no desire to be—only an actor, but I took the problems that were bothering me and used the people on the stage to help me solve my problems, which were mainly how to make an entrance on a stage, how to interpret a part, how to mix improvisation with acting, how to start off a play properly, how to contact and communicate with an audience, how, once you got a laugh, to keep the laugh coming—all the problems an actor would face that I could think of. During the course of this we were dealing with improvisation. Actors would be on the stage doing an improvisation and it turned out to be very bad. I found out that by giving an actor some definite activity to do it would make him better. But it still wasn't very good, so we threw actors who were improvising into the midst of a written scene. What happened was that actors could not go on with the written material. I found that I couldn't go on. I found out that my study had to be deeper. As we made these discoveries, we started throwing away scripts and working more in an improvisational capacity. About that time we came upon a very good improvisation. And out of that improvisation, I said "that would make a heck of a movie." I went on a radio program that night with a friend of mine, Jean Shepherd. While I was there I said I was going to make a movie and that all these people were going to make a movie—wouldn't it be terrific if it could be sponsored by just people. The next day two thousand dollars in dollar bills came in. People from the Army came in and people with equipment came in. Shirley Clarke left some equipment for us. Other people brought in stuff. And they all contributed to this thing. We had two thousand dollars, some equipment, a stage, and actors. As soon as that came in the people started building sets. The picture that came out of this was *Shadows*. So it was, more or less, the desire of a group of people who wanted to accomplish something that started me off in directing, rather than my own personal desires.

AuWerter: Why did you continue to direct?

Cassavetes: I enjoy it because I can write and because I can keep a certain promise to an actor. And because I haven't stopped acting. We made a picture called *Husbands* and I'm in it too. So, it isn't really what kind of a part you have, it's important how well you play it. If you please yourself and you express something—good. As a director you have a responsibility to the picture; there's no doubt that *Husbands* is my picture. But if you ask Ben and Peter, *Husbands* is their picture individually. If you ask Al Ruban or Sam Shaw, the producers—it's their picture.

We all make the film. The making of a film means that people go out and do the best they can to keep a rapport and an understanding and a feeling that what they have to say is more important than the way it's said by any individual.

AuWerter: *Husbands* was the first film in which you directed yourself. Were there any special problems that resulted from this?

Cassavetes: Sure, a lot of special problems. It is very hard to see the scene when you're in it. But it was harder, I think on Peter and Ben, my being in the scene, because I could decide how I was going to play that scene and not worry about the direction of that scene, and they couldn't. The three of us are peers one moment, then suddenly they have to turn to me and say "What do you think?" And they know goddam well I don't know anything more about the scene than they do because I was in it, too. So we learned how to use our instincts. I would say to Peter "how did it go for you?" and he'd say "fine" and then I'd ask Ben and he'd say "fine" and I'd say "fine" and that's the way we'd know.

AuWerter: Would you direct yourself in another picture?

Cassavetes: I never say "never." I thought it was difficult and very strenuous, but I enjoyed it. In *Husbands*, Peter, Ben, and I were the idea of the film—the three of us acting together.

AuWerter: You have written the scripts for the last two pictures you have directed. Is this a pattern that will continue?

Cassavetes: I wouldn't do a picture unless I could write the script. The reason for this is that making a picture or acting in a picture is a very personal thing. I just don't trust anyone else to do what I do. Not because I'm better than anyone else, but because I know that I'll put every last drop of blood I have into it—and not be concerned with the writing.

AuWerter: There isn't a writer, that you know of, who you would like to collaborate with on a picture?

Cassavetes: There are a lot of writers I would love to collaborate with on a picture, but I don't think they would want to collaborate with me. It's a very difficult thing—to say a writer is not important. Somebody writes a good screenplay—it's different from doing the kind of pictures that I do—where the actor is more important than anyone else. I wouldn't be concerned with what a writer felt. I would only be concerned that the actor, who was portraying the writer's character, was comfortable, was happy, and was good. It's a very tough bargain to make with somebody that has an ego and who has been trained in a business where status is everything, to suddenly have a new level of work with new values that say the script doesn't mean a damn thing—rewrite it, do it again, rewrite it, OK, let's improvise it. After improvisation, let's rewrite it again, then let's improvise it. And maybe we won't use anything. Maybe it will be background. I know that I'm willing to do that. I don't know anyone else that is. People say they are, but it's a hell of a lot of work.

AuWerter: How involved do you get in the editing process?

Cassavetes: I think that's a very standard situation. Most editors are very good. On a picture like ours, with editors Peter Tanner and Tom Cornwall—the two English editors that we had here—it was just a matter of their getting used to the material and seeing it. They're in a business where they look at something and then they cut it. They are so expert that they can make it look good. But then they learn that that isn't going to work on a picture like *Husbands*. It's not that they're wrong and I'm right—it's just not going to work. It's a question of their finding that out through a long, hard process.

AuWerter: Does the same apply to your cameraman, your art director, and all the other production people?

Cassavetes: That's right. The best thing that could happen is that everyone be highly involved. Once they're highly involved my job gets easier and easier. It takes a certain amount of time out of your life, to be highly involved, and most people are not willing to give that. Now, that's nothing against them. It's just that it doesn't work if they're not willing to give everything they have, over a long period of time. It's an idea. Either life or death is important to you or it's not. Either the film is life and death to you or it's not. And if it's not, then you're no help. We're saying to ourselves, and this has its own pitfalls too, that we have no limitations on the film. We can say whatever we want to say, whatever pleases us. Now, obviously if nothing pleases you, you ought to get the hell out. But, if something pleases you that can only enhance what we're working on.

AuWerter: Ideally, then, you would like to be able to just concentrate on the acting and the actor?

Cassavetes: In the making of *Husbands*, yes. It's a story about three men, so it would be silly to concentrate on the landscape. It isn't earth's relationship to men that we're talking about, it's men's behavior in terms of themselves.

AuWerter: Do you direct a nonprofessional actor differently from a professional actor?

Cassavetes: No.

AuWerter: When you combine the two in a scene does this create special problems?
Cassavetes: No. I think it's a stimulant.

AuWerter: How do you use improvisation as a part of your directing technique?
Cassavetes: I think you have to define what improvisation does—not what it is. If you don't have a script you don't have a commitment to just saying lines. If you don't have a script, then you take the essence of what you really feel and say that. You can behave more as yourself than you would ordinarily with someone else's lines.

AuWerter: How important is high energy for you as a director?
Cassavetes: I think it's extremely important. For me it's everything. I gain energy by being comfortable. I get drained when I'm uncomfortable. I believe, and I think everyone else around *Husbands* does too, that it's impossible to fail if people are given their head, if people are allowed to do what they know how to do and to do it with some kind of fun. I hate discipline, I despise it. If I walk on a quiet, polite set, I go crazy—I know there's something wrong because somebody has lessened himself in his own estimation and put either me or some actor above himself.

AuWerter: Is taste in any way comparable to energy as a requisite for directing?
Cassavetes: You know, that's a word that's just evaded me all these years.

AuWerter: How much of your directing is therapy?
Cassavetes: Therapy? For whom?

AuWerter: For you or your actors.
Cassavetes: For me, it's all the way. For the actors, I hope it is. It's better than staying home.

AuWerter: Is there any type of picture you wouldn't make?
Cassavetes: Yes, I think probably a musical or a situation comedy.

AuWerter: *Husbands* is your first color picture. Did the change to color affect your directing in any major way?
Cassavetes: It caused me a lot of pain, because I see things in black and white, but Sam Shaw (associate producer of *Husbands*) assured me that the color, if we shot it in a certain way, would look as "black" as anything else I've ever done.

AuWerter: Did being an actor before being a director have any advantages?
Cassavetes: It makes it easier.

AuWerter: Did being an actor before being a director have any disadvantages?
Cassavetes: No. But, being an actor after you're a director has some disadvantages.

AuWerter: Do you see yourself changing with each picture you direct?
Cassavetes: Sure. You have to fight sophistication. Sophistication comes to any-body that has been doing their job for a while. You have to fight knowing, because once you know something, it's hard to be open and creative; it's a form of passiv-ity—something to guard against.

AuWerter: What would you say to young directors who are just starting out?
Cassavetes: Say what you are. Not what you would like to be. Not what you have to be. Just say what you are. And what you are is good enough.

AuWerter: Where do you see yourself in five or ten years?
Cassavetes: I see myself alive.

Dialogue on Film, No. 4: John Cassavetes, Peter Falk

American Film Institute / 1971

From AFI's Harold Lloyd Master Seminar with John Cassavetes © 1971, used courtesy of American Film Institute.

John Cassavetes is one of the few directors to emerge from the underground of independent and/or student film production. His first film, *Shadows*, which he discusses below, placed him in the front ranks of the New York independents loosely clustered around Jonas Mekas's New American Cinema. Cassavetes won the first Independent Film Award given by *Film Culture*.

Eight years later he made *Faces*, which firmly established him as a major talent and, in the process, launched John Marley, Lynn Carlin, and Seymour Cassel, as well as Gena Rowlands (Cassavetes's wife). *Faces* toured the festival circuit and went on to become a commercial success. Since *Faces*, Cassavetes has made two films with major studio backing, *Husbands* and *Minnie and Moskowitz*, in addition to continuing his own career as an actor.

With Cassavetes at this seminar, held in January 1971, was Peter Falk, who worked with Cassavetes in *Husbands*. Fellows and faculty of the Center joined Cassavetes and Falk in a long and often heated discussion of his career.

Just People on the Streets: *Shadows*

Q: How did you come to make *Shadows*? You were in an acting group, weren't you?

John Cassavetes: *Shadows* was an experiment in acting. I was an actor and it happened by accident, the way you get into acting or anything else. I was working in a workshop with a lot of people; one day they were doing an experiment. I said it'd make a terrific film and they started building a set, doing everything, and it was fortunate that I had some money. I went on a radio program and people sent in dollar bills and we started to make this film and we were young. I didn't know anything about filmmaking. I would say, "Print that," only there wasn't anybody there to write that down and we ended up with everything printed.

Those were people I knew and liked, cared for, loved and respected, and they were just people on the streets; people that I associated myself with in my mind. At the end of *Shadows*, the last day of shooting, I couldn't turn on the camera. I was so fed up with doing it because there was no love of the craft or the idea or anything. We're doing this experiment and now it's the last day, nobody's here except McEndree and me. He couldn't turn on the camera and I couldn't turn on the camera and Ben Gazzara was standing there asking, "Are you going to roll this thing or not?" We're just standing there looking at each other. We couldn't turn on this camera because it had been such a hassle.

Q: How did you direct the people in that film?

JC: There was a guy named David Pokitillow that we used a lot; one of the people who hadn't acted before. He played the boyfriend and was a chess player and a violinist. He did the first scene and said, "Listen, that's it." And as you know, that can't be it. "You have got to do this." He said, "No, I don't want to do this." So he promised me he'd do a scene running through the park. He didn't show up. We were standing out there in the park. I knew where he lived and I ran over to his house with a couple of other guys. "John, I'm with a girl for chrissake. I'm not an actor, God, I'm so fat and ugly and I don't want to do this. I don't want to. I just hate it. I hate you." So I said, "David, you have got to do it. If you do it, I swear to God, I'll get you a chess set." I knew he loved chess. "You get the chess set. You come back with the chess set and then I'll do it." So we ran out like a bunch of idiots, got the chess set, came back. He says, "Put it by the door so I can see it." He opens the door and he says, "OK, I'll do it."

So, we get down to the park. There's a scene with Tony Ray and I said, "Hey, you run after him." He said, "I'm not running for anybody." I said, "Please, you can run twenty yards?" He said no. I said, "Please run twenty yards." I'm reduced to nothing. And I'm standing there in the sunlight and the cold and everything and Benny says, "Jesus, man, I'd just deck him." "David, what can I give you?" He said, "A Stradivarius." "I can't give you a Stradivarius. You know I can't afford a Stradivarius, but maybe we can rent it for you." So he ran twenty yards. He said, "That's it." He went home.

Getting People to Do Things

Q: Was working with your friends harder than working with professionals, in a production with a bigger budget?

JC: The whole experience of getting people to do things was incredible. I didn't know what I was doing really. None of us knew what we were doing. When lighting a scene we didn't know what we were doing. We even did the music. I asked Charlie Mingus. I said, "Charlie, would you like to do this?" "Yeah, what is it?" "A film." Charlie said he'd do it for nothing. He worked six months on the music and he wrote a minute and a half's worth of music. I don't know that that's wrong.

He said, "Listen, man, would you do me a favor? You have got to do something for me." "Sure, sure," I say. "Listen, I've got all these cats that are shitting all over the floor. Can you have a couple of your people come up and clean the cat shit? I can't work; they shit all over my music." So we went up with scrubbing brushes and cleaned up the thing. Now he says, "I can't work in this place. It's so clean. I've got to wait for the cats to shit." Finally we get it together to record. So, double session, three hours, double session with the projectionist sitting there and I'm watching. He's got fourteen seconds worth of music. Everybody's saying, "Why don't you just tell Charlie to improvise." All the advice then starts. So then he's got to improvise and he loves to sing and he started to sing and he played. He made everyone switch their instruments. So I said to Charlie, "Charlie, Charlie, it was great; it really sounded great. Everything sounds great. The noise comes out; it really sounds great. It's perfect for the picture." He says, "Man, I got to work six more months." He went away.

Q: Did Mingus finish the film?
JC: Later, I looked for Charlie. He went down to Tijuana. So, I get ahold of Shafi Hadi, and I say, "Shafi, listen, we got to fill in some music here. Do you know where Charlie is? We can't find him. I mean I got to finish this picture. I've been on it for three years now." So he said, "OK, I'll come over. We'll do an improvisation. I've gotta have a hundred bucks." I said, "OK, you've got a hundred." So he came in and he played. It was terrific. He played the story of his life to music. He played for an hour. He said, "Tell me a story. Tell me a story. Tell me a story of myself." I would sit down and tell him a story.

A Bargain to Be More Honest

Q: *Faces* was shot under the same conditions, wasn't it?
JC: *Faces* was very much the same only we had been through all that. So I knew it was going to take a long time. I have a lot of love for actors, so I found every actor I could that was as frustrated as me, every actor that wanted to express something and felt that he was great and had been cheated, and people that just felt there would never be a chance in the world for them. No matter if they worked or didn't work, they were finished.

Q: What kept all those very singularly unique individuals from tearing each other apart?
JC: The bargain was with those people to really be more honest. I enjoyed it. I enjoyed that feeling of cooperation, of working with people that you could respect,

of working with people that loved what they were doing. And the crew loved what they were doing. There were times when George Sims or somebody shooting a scene would be laughing so hard that the camera would shake. This didn't make the actors feel bad; it made them feel good. It made them feel terrific. That was some kind of communication. That third eye was good.

Q: What was your idea for *Faces*?

JC: I wrote it out of a lot of anger and dismay with society. I was unhappy with the way things were going in life. So I wrote this very bitter piece and the actors took it and couldn't make it bitter. That was their insight, their discovery, their feeling for people.

We went up to Toronto to screen the film. When the audience saw the house, they went, "Uhhhh . . ." You could hear it vocally. I started laughing and the people that were with us started laughing, too, because we felt, "Hey, geez, we learned something. We know something now before they see the film that they won't know." Nobody was disappointed that the picture wasn't well received, because all our rewards were in the making of the picture and in what we felt about it. I'll never have an experience like that again in my life, where everything just went perfectly because the people were perfect.

Husbands

Q: How did you come up with *Husbands*?

JC: We started working on *Husbands* as a natural extension of people wanting to continue their lives in work; use what you think you've learned and try to find the subject and deepen it. The only thing you do learn is that you can't go for ten cents and expect to come up with a million. You have to go for everything. You have to go, whether you fail or you don't fail, for what will make us better when we're finished, whether we win or we lose.

Q: What was your approach to the structure of *Husbands*? What was the motivation? What did you start with?

JC: Falk, Gazzara, and myself started with ourselves and a kind of a simple idea of a guy dying; what it would mean to us if one of us, if one of our close friends died. How would we handle it? Our problem was: What did we want to get out of the movie? I'm always delighted, we all are, to make people laugh. I thought, "Oh, Jesus, we've got a comedy that says nothing, absolutely nothing. It's terrific." And then Benny read the script and he said, "Jesus Christ, this is shit. It's about nothing. There's no character, nothing. Who am I? What's in it?" From there until two and a half years later when we finished, Benny would always say, and he still says, "Are you going to make some changes?" And while Peter liked the script, it's harder for me to work with Peter than to work with Ben. When you write something for Ben that he likes, he smiles. He gets excited or he kisses you, or something. With Peter, it's always the same. I say, "What do you think, Peter?" He says, "Uhhh . . . uhhh . . . ehh." Whether he likes it or he doesn't like it, whether it's expressing anything that he wants to say, is very hard to determine.

Q: How did you work out what you were going to do? Did you talk it all out in advance?
JC: From the very beginning we made a pact that we would try to find whatever truth was left in ourselves and talk about that. Sometimes the scenes would reflect things that we didn't like to find out; how idiotic we were, or how little we had to do with ourselves, how uptight we were. We felt that it was important to find a way to have the courage to put that out on a line for whatever it was, even if the picture itself would not be exciting. One of the reasons we did that is because, I think, all three of us felt one thing, and one thing very strongly. That was the idea that there wasn't enough individual expression, bad or good. You have to have the courage to be bad and really express what you want to say. So, throughout the thing, our professionalism got in the way and our egos as well.

Q: That's discipline you're talking about. You're not going to allow yourself to say anything. Is that what you mean by discipline?
JC: As director, I went under the assumption that sooner or later Peter would know what he was doing and sooner or later Ben would know what he was doing, and we'd wait it out until we did know what we were doing. Then, that would be close to what the characters would want to express, for whatever reasons. I was shocked by Peter's choices. I mean, it really surprised me that he would go off in a certain direction.

Everything Is Strength

Q: For *Husbands* what was in the script, and what did you improvise on the set?
JC: What happens is: everything is strength. How much strength do you have? Before you get to improvise on any kind of level, we would have to know that no matter what we did, we would be OK. We had to know the material that well. We could improvise the rehearsal and come out great. We all have the instinct that if we got in front of the camera that that kind of delicate improvisation without any theatricality would lose some of its ease. All of a sudden there would be cameras, cables, guys around, people saying, "We can't move this thing over there," and suddenly the actors would receive very little importance. And you start to fight to preserve what you have and you start pushing, and all of a sudden, it's gone. What had been terribly concentrated in rehearsals would dissipate.

So I found that by writing scenes that we might never use, and writing them again and again and again, that everything that we had written and improvised was, therefore, in our minds, used and usable. We had investigated, then studied it. We knew what we were capable of saying to each other and doing with each other, so we got to the point where we could just give any kind of improvisation. The singing scene, for example, was an improvisation. We had a scene written, but it wasn't very good. It wasn't very clear. It just seemed that these people were there, the extras that had been hired to cover the set. I didn't like the scene that we were doing, so I just said, "Let's improvise this scene here. Put beer on the table and whiskey on the table." I didn't know what we would do. We started and I knew that Peter and Ben would catch on, and that the rest of the people would pick it up, because they weren't going to break the reality.

Q: Did you like working as a director who didn't say anything?
JC: I hated it. It's terrible. It's painful, and terrible, and too disciplined for me. What happened was that, in a scene, it was really an emotional improvisation. I felt that I couldn't gain anything by using direction to make the scene better, telling Peter to all of a sudden behave in a certain way, creating a situation as you usually do in a film. You create a situation. The lack of action was what the picture was about, you see, so if I stimulated action by directing, it would be bad, wrong. Sometimes the guys would just sit there. I mean, somebody dies; I don't know anybody that knows anything to do. I couldn't tell you now what I would do in a situation like that.

Q: *Husbands* has less a cinéma-vérité feel than the earlier films. Did you mean it to be less "realistic"?
JC: Films are usually restricted to realism because films are really a shorthand, the way they have been done. They're a shorthand for living and people understand that shorthand. You have certain labels, like a home run, a double, a single, a triple—baseball jargon—which you use to describe a very powerful scene. Different kinds of things stir the emotional things in you. Films are still predicated on incidents. Incidents are exciting. They set off one thing. You recognize certain incidents, and you go with them. *Husbands* is really a picture about people that feel, but it's done more intellectually than I would like. I get bored seeing two people that are supposed to be in love, who kiss, screw, or whatever they do. I get bored by that because they're only supposed to do those things. I don't really believe that they're doing that, and I couldn't care less. I couldn't care less if people like people, you know, or identify with heroes. Certain times in your life you get bored with yourself. A lot of women will see the drinking scene and they're bored the first second they see it. They're bored the first second there's

a drunk there. They don't like the idea of people revealing themselves. If people can't reveal themselves heavily, then there is nothing to identify with. If the men are not exciting, there's nothing for people to identify with, because we all want to be excited. I think the picture is about people just being what they are, and that's good enough. If that's not good enough, then maybe as a movie it will fail.

A Thin Line of Feeling

Q: How do you justify this to an audience?

JC: There is a thin line of feeling in the film. You take the script, if you ever read the script, or you see the movie, and if you don't want to be connected with the fact that something is going on with these guys, then it is long and involved and maybe boring. It was difficult to know how much to lead an audience, because we didn't want to lead them at all. We didn't want to justify these guys' behavior in terms of the story that we were trying to tell. We wanted to just let it go saying that the feeling would carry the story, the feeling underlying the fact that I knew these guys and cared about the guy that died. I knew they cared about each other, and I knew that they cared about their wives. We in the film were always putting ourselves up, discovering some things about us that we wouldn't ordinarily know. That's something that you wouldn't ordinarily see in a film. No one in an audience would have time nor interest in it, and that was our interest.

Q: Did you have the drinking scene in the bar completely worked out?

JC: I had a basic idea that it would go off in a certain direction. The point was only what we, as characters, were feeling and not what the other people in the scene or in the audience were going to feel. Whether they felt or not, it would be a victory for us. What we were feeling was: we wanted people to be involved with our lives and actually we didn't want them to be involved with our lives, but we wanted what we were feeling to be important at the moment.

They Were Bugged about the Money

Q: What was your relationship with your cameraman?

JC: We started out the picture with a terrific cameraman named Aldo Tonti from Italy. He is one of the world's greatest cameramen. He shot a lot of the early Fellini things. He's really a terrific guy. We had some problems with him because he was afraid of the Italian people who had put up the money with us, and he wasn't himself on the picture and couldn't make any headway there. It was a New York crew. We had a lot of problems because the only way we could shoot the picture for the money we had was to quit at 4 o'clock every day, and there was no overtime coming in so the crew was really hostile to us. I mean, not personally hostile. They were bugged about the money.

The crew didn't know what we were doing or understand our attitudes. We used every moment to increase our friendship. So we would put ourselves up against the crew and never have lunch with them, never talk to them. I never said a word to the crew the whole time I was there. Not one word.

Q: You must have said something. For instance, if Falk went a little to the right, did you say to the cameraman, "Just stay with the action?" Or did you give them freedom?

JC: Oh, no. The operator, the second-unit cameraman who became the cameraman, was Vic Kemper. Vic happened to be a terrifically inventive cameraman. I like him personally; he's really good. Before Vic became the cameraman, he was a second-unit cameraman. When I saw his first work, I could just feel by the way he was moving the camera and the confidence that he had, that I wouldn't have to tell him anything. I didn't have to tell him anything on the close-ups in the bar. He just shot everything by himself. He worked out his own camera, and the only thing I said to him was, "Feeling." Sometimes you have an idea of what you would really like to see. I just have a general idea. I don't usually look into the camera, because I look at the light. If I like the light of what is happening, then I don't care where the camera is particularly. I don't think it matters in the long run. I liked it low because we were dealing with three short guys. We had the camera low so we wouldn't look like total dwarfs.

Q: Shouldn't a film reflect the director's picturization, the visual image of it he has in his head?

JC: It's not really interesting to me, at least, to set up a camera angle. At some points in the film you really want to take the camera and break it for no reason except that it's just an interference and you don't know what to do with it. It's like putting the top on a can that is bent. You can't really do anything with it. The most difficult part of working on a film like this is that the opinions of the crew really affect the people in front of the screen, and sometimes they don't see anything happening. They get despondent. You can feel them loosen up. You can feel you're losing the thing. The only strength that we had was in the three of us.

No Chance, Baby, No Laughter

Q: Could you tell how you utilized that, in structuring the beautiful scene between Peter Falk and the old woman in the casino?

JC: There was a feeling between Peter and me that we were going to kill each other. So we had to be nice to each other when we were working with one another as actors. We finished a huge, long sequence between two women, previous to Peter going over to that woman. Peter said, "Godammit, this has gotta be written cuz that last scene was improvised. Gimme something to say here." So I took that lady and Peter and I wrote a scene and gave it to him. The secretary wrote it out and gave it to Peter and to the lady, and she looked at it. I don't know how she got it, but somehow, I don't know if it was by osmosis, but it came.

That was a terrible sequence. Peter was all right, but how could she catch up? She was just sitting there. She was out of place. She didn't know what to expect. All the camera crew and everybody else was looking at this woman. What was going to happen? She had a few lines, and she had to, in a sense, be romantic. Peter played the scene with her. It was very good, and she was very good. I would say things like, "Look at that face."

Q: What kind of direction did you give her?
JC: Sometimes it's utter and total cruelty to elicit something pretty out of somebody. You have to be cruel to somebody sometimes, but it is only cruel in some kind of a social bullshit way. I mean, we're all there to get something good. The woman was tight. She didn't know what was expected of her, and it was too late for her to find out in the course of the filming. I would say terrible things to her, just awful things. She would fight them off like a lady. She reached a point where she could do everything by herself. She was grateful for that attitude of not giving a shit of what anybody else thought, because everything bad had already happened. From there on in, she just started to play. She was herself, which she had to be.

Q: Was she an actress?
JC: No. She was a ballet dancer, a ballet dancer who . . . it's so crazy. You see somebody sitting there and anybody can see it, you know.

You see that woman sitting there and you've got to have her in the scene. It's terrific for Peter to try to pick up that woman. It's right that he would pick her up, because she is the safest woman in the place. It was very easy for him to talk to her. Peter was all right, because he was really comfortable. He was more comfortable in that scene than in a lot of other scenes, because it was right. The situation was right. He would go over and talk to that woman. She's a terrific woman.

Q: The sequence was brutal, in a way, brutalizing of that woman.
JC: What I see in that scene is the brief moment of loneliness for a woman. I find it very beautiful. I find that woman very beautiful, because she still cares. She still tries. She's not cool, but I'd just as soon be with her as a person, than a lot of other people that were on the picture that didn't put out as much. I interfered, directed, because I wanted something to mean something. To me this was a rich old lady that expressed well in a way what I'd like to see expressed.

Q: But you must realize that she expresses a lot of other things to the audience.

JC: Not to me. She expressed a rich old lady who was old and wrinkled. Her belly was wrinkled and she wanted to be beautiful. That is what she expresses.

Q: She also expresses a very coarse type of comedy to the audience. The audience isn't laughing at any sort of real value. They're laughing at a programmed sort of caricature.

JC: How do you know that? Let's let people laugh at what they want to laugh at. Why shouldn't they laugh? You made a judgment already. You made a judgment that people are not supposed to laugh at a serious thing. Listen. I've had people close to me, die, and I giggled. No one is going to tell me about it. You can't tell me how I feel. You can't tell that. You see that woman. Maybe you don't like her being made fun of by the audience that's sitting there, but it's a healthy thing. It's healthy to laugh at somebody. Do you know why people don't laugh at people? Because they are too high and mighty to laugh. They don't like them enough to invest their time to laugh, because if you laugh at somebody, you know you're going to have to be connected with them. You are going to have to put some time in with them. You know that you are going to have to truly like those people. The truth of the matter is that nobody can afford to laugh at anybody. That's why some fucking psychologist comes along and says, "Don't laugh at him." When friends get together, they laugh at each other. When enemies get together, no chance, baby. No laughter.

The Picture Starts Taking Over

Q: Did the scene where Ben confronts his wife and his mother-in-law cause you much trouble?

JC: Yes. It was staged, but it caused a lot of worry. But it was a situation that you knew had to work. I realized in making the picture, that it was more difficult dealing with three guys and what three guys wanted, than it was dealing with one guy and what he wanted. I was constantly aware of the structural problems. One of us had a turn, and then another, and then another. Somehow the picture had to start taking over so that nobody had any more turns. What is happening evolves out of the action, but there is no specific importance to individual incidents. This scene with Ben evolved because we knew that people would say, "Gee, you never saw one wife." That just kept ringing in my mind. I didn't want people to approach me on the street and say, "Isn't it wonderful? You never saw a wife in that." That's kind of a nightmare. We decided to show the one wife. To do that we had to come up with some kind of relationship that would be meaningful for the other two guys. We wrote a very quick scene. We got the actors in, and got a stage. It was all very stagy. I knew that it would pay off once he choked the mother-in-law.

Q: Did you have problems in keeping yourself and Ben and Peter from running away with a scene?

JC: Peter had a great number of problems integrating my ideas with his ideas. I hate "stars" where that means an actor is so involved with a character that he says, "Take the scene. Make it mine, and make it good. Move the audience, and make them laugh. Once you get them going, don't let them off the hook." Peter was looking to grab that audience and make them sit up so they were going with him.

He couldn't take them and push them anywhere. He couldn't take the audience and grab them and tie them into a knot, because that would just be leaving them there. The next time he appeared, they would say, "What happened to him?" It wouldn't be part of a structure made up of three guys. The whole thing was working with three guys. The three of us really like to grab a scene and do something with it. But, we had to work more like amateurs. We had to be really involved with each moment, without ever allowing anybody to grab onto that moment and make it their own.

There Was No Character, There Was Me

Q: Would you do a film like *Husbands* again?

Peter Falk: I would like to do a film like *Husbands* again. I would be curious to know whether or not, if I did it again, I could be better. A lot of the time, I didn't understand it. I didn't understand it, and I don't think I gave enough, because I couldn't zero in on exactly what was going on and how to do it. Maybe the next time I wouldn't either, but I think I would have a better chance. We all have instincts about beginnings, middles, and ends. We know what a climax is and what a dramatic moment is. It's very hard to get rid of that thinking. It's very hard not to go with it, to be able to rely on and trust something that is smaller, subtler, but more genuine. It's very hard also to be tangled with a preconceived idea; to just start a scene and see what will happen, what will come out of it and without imposing on it some idea that you have. That is hard to do and I didn't do it. I did it sometimes. I think as the film went on, I did it more, but in the beginning I was hanging onto an old way. I can't understand John. I don't understand him.

Q: What were your preconceived ideas of that character?

PF: I'm not going to be very helpful to you, because I gotta tell you that I didn't have any preconceived ideas. I was just confused. Now, did you understand that? Yes, I was confused and a lot of the confusion came from myself. I wasn't willing to settle on anything, to settle on whatever happened, whatever I was feeling at the moment. I didn't trust him. I didn't think that it was important enough, or I didn't think that it was theatrical enough, or I couldn't put it together with something that was going to come later. I'm used to seeing the whole part laid out, so I know where I am going.

Q: Were you playing a character? Were you thinking in terms of another person?
PF: There was no character. There was me.

He'd Fall Down Laughing: Actors and Directors

Q: How do you relate to guys like Aldrich or Siegel? Do you see what you are trying to do is put more life inside a picture than most films have?
JC: If I'm just a straight actor, I just try to do the best job I can. Sometimes you can't and sometimes you can. It really has a lot to do with what the director feels about you personally and how you balance chemically. With Aldrich, everything that I did, he would fall down laughing. He'd put his arm around me, and I just knew that he liked me. He'd say, "Do this." I'd say, "You want me to do this?" I knew that everything that I'd say would be right for him. I worked with Polanski and he's very delicate and impersonal. I don't function best that way. I don't function with him personally, and we didn't get along. It's not really in the work, but basically it's people.

Q: As an actor, how do you feel about your relationship with the director?
JC: I think if you are an actor, first of all, you are set aside from a director. You basically don't like directors but the director shouldn't worry about that. That's number one. Any director who worries about whether or not an actor likes him is crazy, because it's never going to happen. It will happen as the result of being finished, seeing the work, and then if he has the time, he'll say, "OK." Half of the problem that a director has is he's not only trying to adjust to the actors, but to the technicians, to the front office, and to the financial problems that are existent. He doesn't address himself to the problem of what it is he's trying to say.

I don't think it really has anything to do with liking somebody. I've liked directors that I thought were terrible. You can go out and have drinks with them, and they are really nice guys. You feel sorry for them because they don't have more talent. You hope they can work more, because their livelihood depends upon it. I think a guy like Polanski is enormously talented as a director. I don't like him personally, but I'd like to work with him. If there was some way to work with a guy and not like him personally, then I'd work with him anytime.

Actors are your arms. They are part of you. Now, if your stomach erupts on you, then you treat it kindly. You don't punch yourself in the stomach, so you don't punch the actors. If an actor has a problem, it could be one of three things. It could be an ego problem, an emotional problem, or it could be an acting problem. It's really impossible for you to tell, because it is impossible for the actor to tell. When you are working with actors, you will have no problem if you can resolve that you are working in the same direction. Peter and I really disagreed, not on what the character was or wasn't, but in the way of the work, how the work was working. Should you stand there until something happens? Or should you have something, and then determine yourself how that should happen? I am strong-minded and say, "No, it's got to be the other way. It's got to be: stand there until something happens." He'll go along with me, not because he agrees, but because I am willing to put my money up. I won't back down on that and when I do, he hits the ceiling. I did a couple of times in the picture. He said, "Let's have another take," and I said, "No." I would tell him, "It's too expensive. Thirty thousand dollars every shot. Screw it. It's not important. It's great." He had a right to get mad at me. I wouldn't get mad back at him. But, I am glad that I said, "No," because I didn't want to spend that loot. We could handle it in a different way, but that wasn't his problem. He won't be understanding of that. I'm glad that he hated me, because I was hateable.

A Slave to What You Want

Q: Your communication with your director is indirect, then?

JC: If, as a director, you want something strongly enough, the actor will see that more than he'll see you. He's not interested or concerned with you. He's interested and concerned with what you want, and he's a slave to what you want. You can't divorce yourself from what the director wants. It's impossible. Even if you hate him, you can go home and say, "Ahhhhh, I wanted it done the other way," but you know the minute he suggests a way, then that's it.

PF: Whatever you say as a director, that actor hears it. It's always going to be in his mind.

JC: No matter what kind of jerk he is. The director could be an absolute imbecile. If he says it, we are so trained and oriented that we've got to do that. Otherwise, we fail. In directions I try to break that down in actors. I don't want the actor to listen to me, because I know if I say something wrong, they'll listen to it. Every time I gave a direction on *Husbands*, it was wrong. I knew that it was wrong just as fast as the actor knew it, but it sounded right theoretically. It was my attempt to try to have an actor do something better. But I'll never be as close as a director to my part as I will as an actor, and I'll never have the same problems. I'm going to tell you how to behave, how you should sit? That's what it really boils down to: where to put your feet, where to put your hands. It is better if the actor has an overall understanding of what he's doing or what you are trying to do. You can talk to him as you talk to a writer, as you would talk to another person about a character. You sit down and you tell the actor a story of who that actor is and what he is. Then you can say to him, "Hey, listen. When you are the parking lot attendant, and you come up, don't be hostile there." He understands it in the simplest terms. So, that's a direction, but it's not a direction. The actor is going to go off base. He's not real for himself, because you wouldn't have said anything that convinced him.

Directing as a Lifestyle

Q: Do you think there is any way that films can be made in this country where you can get a crew that sees it as more than just a job?

JC: If you are interested in films in this country, you want to be a director. It's like in music. You really would like to write your own stuff if you could. I think film and music are very close, since what you are putting down is really more important than just interpreting somebody else's material. But I think now there just isn't enough regard or interest in the beauty of the technical work interrelated with an overall story. I think that everybody learns how to take a camera apart, how to reset it, how to load it, and how to put in your sound sync. But, what is the relation, what is the technical responsibility of the cameraman, of the focus puller, and of the various members of the crew making a picture in the overall sense?

Q: When you direct now, how do you relate to your crew?

JC: Directors don't really get along with a crew, because usually a crew isn't involved, unless it's the way you work where you're working with people. I walk in as a director and meet my cameraman. He's got his crew and that is his army. The guy in the sound department has his army, and the painter has to check with the cameraman to see whether to put shiny walls over there. At what point can I have some kind of a rapport with the operator? The guy is so conditioned that he has to look to his boss to find out if what he is doing is OK, or he has to look to the studio to find out if it is OK. I think this holds true in terms of union jobs. There is no guy that doesn't say, "Geez, I shouldn't be shooting this, because I am the Director of Photography, but I think it will be OK." He will do a wonderful job, bravo, and you say, "Oh, bullshit, if you are that good, you should be picking up that camera all of the time. What are you waiting for? Somebody to tell you that?" I loved working on *Faces* in terms of the crew, because they were all actors and nobody had anything to lose by being a bad cameraman. The guy that we ultimately got to be the operator, George Sims, was terrific. When he didn't understand something, or he didn't like it or didn't feel it, he wouldn't have any resentment. He would just say, "I don't feel it. Maybe you could do it better?"

There are cameramen who have an awful lot to teach people. It's very tough to work with key lights. It's a craft that a lot of Hollywood cameramen really learned, and they do it well. A lot of new guys can work with soft lights, and that's all they can work with. You get into a big area. It's a very tough way to work with soft lights. Those guys can be terrific, but they have their money to think of. They get fifteen hundred dollars a week and one thing or another. They didn't want to lose their status symbol. What has it got to do with the picture though?

Q: Why couldn't you have done *Husbands* in the same way that you had worked before?

JC: I really find that you can't work twice with technicians because they think they know what you are doing. It's different with Bergman. They're in a little company. They have a company and they prefer to work that way. I like the mystery of working with new people all the time. Half of the thing is seeing whether you can communicate.

Each person on a crew has to have his emotional reflection of what he has done every day. It isn't a real emotional reflection. It's just the strata of society we're in which demands a drink afterwards, a good morning, a certain behavior, and a certain demeanor that would indicate that you like everybody. Eventually, you walk in and you don't like everybody. You just simply get tired, not of people, but of not functioning on a level that is meaningful to you.

I like the people. I love making pictures, and I try to avoid anything that makes it impossible. I always lose that way. I never win. I suppose you get something out of it if you realize what you are doing is crap. You make that concession to yourself, and yet I can't really do that.

Go with Other People

Q: It's been hard, but you have made it.

PF: I wish I had enough sense when I was beginning. I didn't know anything. If I was just starting and I was in an Institute like this, I'd just get the people that I liked, and I'd go out and make a film. I would say it is more fun to get together with yourselves and make something by working that way. People drift off and they start on their own. Some stick. You can pick up others, but start right here. Don't go over there. Start right here. Go with other people.

JC: You see, there really have been no good films made. David Lean, with the exception of *Ryan's Daughter*, has made consistently good Hollywood films. He's done some terrific editing and experimentation through his career. There's nothing wrong with Ernst Lubitsch or any of the comedy directors who are free and loose. That system doesn't really exist anymore where you have more than one opportunity. The problem today is continuity. If you go into a major studio, you can be George Stevens or anybody else. If you make a losing picture, you are through and you know that.

Q: You have managed to function in that system.

JC: You have got to be more uptight, even if you can function in that system. I made *Husbands* and I know goddam well I've got to sell it too. I'm not going to get another chance to make a picture. It's too expensive. You con people and you lie to them. You try to keep a little part of yourself when somebody says to you, "You figure it's the greatest picture ever made?" You try to keep a little part of yourself alive.

It's the same thing if you are a cameraman behind a camera with a director who is uptight. They know the guy's uptight. What can they do about it? Can they say, "Look, you're uptight. Relax?" They are going to have to live with it afterwards. They will go out and have a drink, go home, argue with their wives, and be unhappy.

Q: What alternatives are there to that system?

JC: There doesn't seem to be any solution within that framework whereby people could say, "I am going into the distribution movie business for money," and we approach it behind the scenes as an art. We can't.

Soon your tastes change. You can't combine the two styles. You are not expressing what you want to say and that becomes a lie. You are making an entertainment that will suit the people that are producing the film, the studio itself. They say that they know what people like. They are full of shit. They don't know any more than I do. I don't even know what I like. You only know what you like. Some guy that is introverted, who has a chauffeured limousine pick him up and drive him to a projection room, he's going to tell me what people like? Jesus, he was never in Times Square. My hostility toward him is for making that statement, not for him personally. It's for maintaining that he's the head, but I know that he's the head only as long as he can convince everyone there's a mystique and a mystery about what he does.

A Small Cop-Out Which Kills You

Q: You seem to be saying that the system is a monolith, and it corrupts everybody in it?

JC: That is what you are really combatting. As a result of that system, you are combatting the guy on the camera. It could be your best friend. Somebody says, "Charlie, what do you think?" And your best friend says, "Well, I think this." You look to your friend, and your friend says, "Well, I don't know." You know that he copped out on you. That's a small cop-out, but that kills you. You are working in a vacuum. You are really working in a vacuum. Peter goes and rewrites all the scripts he tries, but it is like quicksand. The minute he rewrites it, they rewrite it again. And you are not just talking about some continuity. They don't care. They may be rewriting him because it's too long. In most places it is. They have a time schedule. He doesn't understand it and it isn't done by saying, "Look, Peter, do you think you could take this and shorten it down because we have to do it in this amount of time?" No, they cut it. They put him over in a corner and say, "Stand over there, Peter. It's going to be beautiful. Don't worry."

It's also a matter of economics. That's everything, isn't it? Is it any different in schools or colleges? Why do you think all the problems exist? They exist because somebody goes up there and says, "Wouldn't it be terrific if we had a film department?" They say, "No film department." How do you buck the system? What are they going to do? Quit? You are going to offend some guy with a pipe standing there.

Q: I think all of us here want to go out and make a film, and yet there is this insurmountable wall we somehow have to crack. After you've made these films, what are some of your ideas about getting over that wall or around it?

JC: If you have to make a film, you have to make a film. I don't know how, but you'll find a way to make it if you have to. If you have to be a director, it means taking on a lot of problems. But the wrong way to go about it is to go to a great deal of trouble to do one little simple thing, that you should go directly to. I found myself in the position of forming a distribution company. In my mind I have raised $118 million in one day. But what I want to do is just make one film for $50,000. I don't think any of us really have the answer to that. I don't have the answer. I got a film that I'd like to do and I'm in the position of having to determine what is important in making that film: making it, selling it, or having people view it? I have got to deal with Universal. It kills me to have to make that deal. It is more important to make my picture. Let them bury it. Let them sink it. I don't care what they do with it. I have got to say that to myself. I earned the right to at least have my cut. I can get my own print so I'll always have my film. I know I am saying I've given up, but I'm really content at this time with being able to do that. I am still thrilled at the idea of being able to make a film. My thrill is something out of nothing, some little idea that pleases me or stirs me, or some place that I can put myself up, or other people can put themselves up to make something good.

What We Said Was What We Said

Q: Working as we must, we are all in danger constantly of having everything we've tried to do taken away.

JC: I got a wire the other day and a letter from Columbia saying, "Would you please cut *Husbands* because we are really losing the audience, especially in the singing scene. They can't take that and the vomiting scene. Thirty to fifty people a night go up and ask for their money back during that sequence." My answer to them at that time was: "Buy me out of the film and I'll be happy to cut ten minutes out of the film for you. Just give me a lot of money and I'll cut that out." A lot of people legitimately feel that that scene is too long. It really doesn't make any difference whether somebody likes it or doesn't like it, and whether they would like the film longer or not. I personally liked the film longer, but it really doesn't make any difference, because what we said was what we said. I don't believe in anything as a work of art. The film is some kind of an expression that people can either relate to or not. They either like it or they don't like it. It either means something to them or it doesn't. Emotions don't make any sense except that they are true— they are there all the time.

Movie Journal

Jonas Mekas / 1971

From the *Village Voice*, December 23, 1971, 63–64. Reprinted by permission of Jonas Mekas.

The screening of John Cassavetes's *Shadows*, late in December 1958, became an occasion from which the rise of the New American Cinema is usually dated. I still remember the excitement some of us felt that late night, at the Paris Theatre. We stood there, in the lobby, and we didn't want to leave. Independent film in America, known at that time as experimental film, had been going strong since 1943, but it was beginning to need a fresh impulse. The screening of *Shadows* and, a few months later, *Pull My Daisy* (Robert Frank was there too, at the screening of *Shadows*) started moving the strange forces which grew and spread and exploded into what eventually became known as underground film.

John Cassavetes went his own way. He went to Hollywood. But not totally. Two of his six films have been produced by others—*Too Late Blues* (Paramount) and *A Child Is Waiting* (Stanley Kramer); *Shadows*, *Faces*, *Husbands*, and now *Minnie and Moskowitz* were produced by Cassavetes himself. I am particularly interested in his last three films. *Faces*, *Husbands*, and *Minnie and Moskowitz* form one of the most original trilogies in the contemporary American cinema. All three films explore a rarely touched area of the middle-aged man and woman. Cassavetes documents their emotions, their thoughts, their relationships. A unique chronicle of the contemporary, average American middle-class man and woman emerges.

On the occasion of the release of *Minnie*, Cassavetes came to town and I asked him a few questions.

Jonas: I just saw your latest film, *Minnie and Moskowitz*. I liked it very much. It may not be a perfect film, but it is original, it is honest, it's about real people. They are very sad, lonely people. They are so lonely that they attach themselves to anybody, and they cling without any understanding of the relationship. Their relations are so distorted by their loneliness that everything becomes exaggerated, unreal, brutal. They can't even talk to each other, they have to shout, or they have to brutalize each other—that seems to be the only way they know how to reach each other.

Cassavetes: Like they have become invisible, and nobody can see or reach their real selves any longer.

Jonas: Anyway, the relationships are very intense in your films. All your films have been built on relationships, and not on plots or situations. Of course, you have various situations there, but it's through these small personal relationships that they clash, that they open themselves, reveal themselves. But I have heard people say that your films are "stupid," or that they make people look more stupid than they really are. Why do you think they say that?

Cassavetes: They say so because it's very difficult for some people to feel, or to see themselves in a bad form. I think that people in films are expected to be heroes even with the anti-hero situation going on for years and years in literature. People expect too much from themselves, they want to look great. We always look for great causes, for answers.

Jonas: Your protagonists don't seem interested in causes or ideas. They are interested only in themselves, their own lives, emotions. But people think emotions are stupid, they hide them.

Cassavetes: But in my opinion, these people and these small emotions are the greatest political force there is. These small emotions, these character disagreements are of vital necessity, and I see it disappearing. Ten, fifteen years ago people could disagree without killing each other. They could disagree and still like the person with whom they disagreed, on a different level, on a human level—no matter how different their lives were. But now that human level has disappeared and there is only one level of agreement, and that's lifestyle. If your lifestyle is like my lifestyle, then we like each other; if your lifestyle is not like my lifestyle then we can see nothing in each other.

Jonas: In *Minnie*, did you indicate to your actors what characters they should play or did they make up their own?

Cassavetes: I wrote the characters, and they filled them in. And then we worked on them together. It was quite a detailed script.

Jonas: Ever since *Shadows* came out, your name is always connected with the terms "spontaneity," "improvisation." People are very confused about what those terms mean, they think anything goes. To what extent do you use improvisation and what's the meaning of it, for you?

Cassavetes: As a technique, it's useless. As a way to achieve an individuality in a characterization it's very, very constructive. I give somebody some lines, and the interpretation must be their own. And if that interpretation means those lines must change, as they want to express themselves, then I'd change the lines or let them improvise their own lines. But not as a technical device. It's a device to really allow some individual to express an individual idea, thought, or emotion. And then I take another person and let him or her have an individual idea or emotion. And that makes the conflict. Any conflict that would arise would be two people feeling absolutely different about the same emotion. So that you build a world of individual characters rather than characters that look all the same and where the lines can be interchangeable. How could a person like Seymour whose whole lifestyle is one way, suddenly change? Because I want him to change? You can't change him. He has to change gradually.

Jonas: Was there a progression through your films in how much improvisation you allowed? What about *Faces*?

Cassavetes: There was none in *Faces*, none at all. I felt we were on totally new grounds. *Shadows*, it was an experiment. It dealt with youth, and there is no restriction on youth. But *Faces* deals with middle age, and in middle age there are restrictions. There is restriction in behavior. A totally free behavior would become an indulgence in a picture like this, it would become destructive. So that to reveal middle age in all its complexities and simplicity and frustration, it must be more rigid, even in the acting itself. At least the first time that we did it, it had to be rigid. And after a month of shooting we could really relax, much more than in the beginning—we threw out the first month of shooting. Then it became a self-imposed discipline. The actors disciplined themselves to stay close to their own intentions, without too much variance.

Jonas: They really had to give themselves out. Because the whole film, all of its visual material, its content was not so much in lines but in their just being as they were. I thought it was a unique film, because you can't create that kind of content by lines or situations. It's a very difficult kind of film to make, difficult content to get on film. It's either you pull it out of them or not, through their faces, through their laugh, expressions, attitudes. And many people I spoke to thought that was an easy kind of film to do.

Cassavetes: I was brutal on that picture. I was brutal to the actors. Because I had to get it, to me it was really the most important thing. It was important, because we had already gone through the experimentation. So we spent another four years on *Faces*, working on it. I insisted on the characters revealing themselves much more obviously than characters usually would reveal themselves in any other movie.

Jonas: Usually directors prefer understatement in actors, in cinema. But you seem to work with overstatements, in your last three films.
Cassavetes: That's right. Almost heavy-handed, and repetitious in its emotional quality.

Jonas: And it's that aspect that the smart people take for "stupidity." In other words: they miss the very essence of your work. I also think they don't like the fact that you deal with middle age.
Cassavetes: Because in this country, people die at twenty-one. They die emotionally at twenty-one. Maybe even younger, now. For those of us who are lucky not to die at twenty, we keep on going, and my responsibility as an artist is to help people get over twenty-one. I wanted to make *Faces*, for instance, because I was really angry at our age and especially at those adults who without thinking go to discotheques, without thinking join into anything that is fashionable, and without any understanding. I wanted to show the inability of people to communicate; what small things will do to people; how people can't handle certain things that they hear and read in newspapers, see in films; and how, when they are not prepared to think with their own minds, and to feel, how all this can become tragic circumstances.

I wrote *Minnie* because I didn't think that two people can get married anymore. Myself, I couldn't understand why two people would get married today. So that the making of this film was an investigation to me of something that I don't understand. And then I get actors to work on that idea, saying, how do two people get married today? Is it possible? So I talk to Seymour, and it's up to him really to find some kind of truth and honesty in himself, away from all the programmed behavior.

Jonas: One thing I like about *Minnie and Moskowitz* is the character ambiguity of your people. They are never too clearly bad or good, sympathetic or unsympathetic.
Cassavetes: I feel that judgments have to be left to the audience. It's beyond the theatrics of screen personalities, I think. The majority of ten thousand people that I've come into contact with, personally in my life, I've never seen anyone go and blow somebody's head off. So why should I make films about them? But I have seen people destroy themselves in the smallest way, I've seen people withdraw, I've seen people hide behind political ideas, behind dope, behind the sexual revolution, behind fascism, behind hypocrisy, and I've myself done all these things. So I can understand them and I say, Jesus, I like this person even though I know he is a s.o.b., you know, I love him and I can't help him, it's his personality and his style that I like.

I don't care if people like our films or not. As long as I can make these films and say what I want and work with people I love and who are not afraid to express themselves, whether it's popular or not. What we are saying is so gentle. It's gentleness. We have problems, we have terrible problems, but our problems are human problems, they are not financial problems. This whole culture, there is only one art in America, and that's money. Raising money, and business. That's what everyone is interested in, in this art, the art of making money, screwing somebody and making profit. We went to the Pratt Institute the other night, and one of the kids said, "16mm is not for me," you know? It's not for me! We want to get out of this! We want to get into the thing! I make films for the big studios, but I've never told them the truth. I've never been nice to them, and the understanding is there that I go my way and they go their way. If I can't do what I want with them, I'll go to 16mm, and if I can't do it there I'll go to 8mm.

Jonas: What contemporary American movies do you like?
Cassavetes: As a director, I like Elaine May.

Jonas: Elaine May? Who is Elaine May?
Cassavetes: She only made one picture, *A New Leaf*. She did it at Paramount. She is terrific. She directed it and appeared in it. I am going to make a film with her, as an actor. Another director I like very much is Marty Scorsese, he did *Street Scenes* and *Who's That Knocking at My Door*. I like also Don Siegel, I think he is very pure. I like Robert Aldrich, he is very good with actors. I like Dennis Hopper also, he is an experimenter. He may be crazy, but he at least tries to say something, even if you don't agree with it. And Bogdanovich, he is very good. I also like this new picture, *Made for Each Other*, by Robert Bean, I think it's excellent. It's his first film. And then there is Tim Carey who has been making a film now for seven years, splicing it together, and still reshooting, out of money, and he never gives up. You talk to Tim, and he says: "I don't care anything about anybody, I want to make my films, because that's it, that's all I want to do, to sit by myself in my room with my 16mm moviola, have the film break, and me fix it like a baby, and smell it, and walk on it, and break it if I want to, but that's what I want to do, to take these people and give them life, that's all I care about in life."

John Cassavetes, Gena Rowlands, Peter Falk on Movies, Madness, and Myths

Dick Adler / 1974

From *Viva* (December 1974), 61–63, 90. Reprinted by permission of Dan Adler

John Cassavetes, the tousled, boyish, forty-four-year-old actor who stars in such high-budget entertainments as *Rosemary's Baby* and *The Dirty Dozen* to help finance his own much less commercial projects, has directed seven films. His first was *Shadows* in 1961, which won an award at Venice as a "breakthrough in American cinéma-vérité," and the latest is *A Woman Under the Influence*, shown in October at the New York Film Festival and soon to be nationally released.

A native New Yorker and son of a Greek-born Harvard graduate who made and lost several millions in various business ventures, Cassavetes thought he'd be a sports announcer until he began reading the plays of Robert Sherwood at Colgate University. After that he worked in summer stock and pounded the Broadway pavements before winning the role of a moody bullfighter on TV's *Omnibus*, which launched his acting career in 1959. He went on to act in over one hundred TV shows.

As a director, Cassavetes isn't everyone's cup of gin. A critic said about *Faces*—shot in eight months for forty thousand dollars and then edited for four years—that it was "so blunt and relentless that one is clubbed to the floor." Another spoke of his "assertive and unyielding style." Both *Husbands* and *Minnie and Moskowitz* received, among generally good notices, a few complaints about their rough edges and apparent lack of coherence.

But one thing which no critic has ever accused Cassavetes of being is like any other director. "Johnny has more energy and enthusiasm than anyone I know," says a friend who has watched his career develop over the past ten years. "He's kept that enthusiasm—or is it naïveté—even when he's being kicked in the face." The body of work he considers his own—the five films he conceived and wrote and financed himself—is unique in theme and execution, a continuing private vision of the relationships between men and women. And even his two "studio" movies, *Too Late Blues* and *A Child Is Waiting*, which were taken away from him and mauled by the people who put up the money, have occasional flashes of that vision.

Three of Cassavetes's films have starred an exceptionally talented and beautiful woman named Gena Rowlands, who since 1958 has been the director's wife and mother of their three children—son Nicholas, fourteen, and daughters Xan (for Alexandra), eight, and Zoe, three.

The Wisconsin-born Miss Rowlands met Cassavetes at the Academy of Dramatic Arts, where they were both studying acting. When she graduated, she played the lead opposite Edward G. Robinson in Paddy Chayefsky's Broadway hit *Middle of the Night*. She has since starred in countless TV shows and movies—always winning kudos for her original and luminous performances.

In *Faces* she played an expensive prostitute; in *Minnie and Moskowitz* she was a traditional romantic suffering from culture shock. And in *A Woman Under the Influence* she takes on what she considers her most demanding role—a wife and mother driven mad by her life.

The actor who plays Gena Rowlands's husband in *A Woman Under the Influence* is Peter Falk, now best known as the star of NBC's *Columbo* series. Born in Ossining, New York, in 1927, Falk took a master's degree in public administration at Syracuse University before he switched to acting. He studied with Eva Le Gallienne and worked at the Circle in the Square. He and Cassavetes first worked together as actors in a gangster melodrama called *Machine Gun McCain* and went on to team up with Ben Gazzara for Cassavetes's *Husbands*. Two seasons ago he starred on Broadway in Neil Simon's *Prisoner of Second Avenue*—his performance as the half-crazed New Yorker being described as "bravura." While *A Woman Under the Influence* was being made, Falk and Cassavetes also managed to star for director Elaine May in an upcoming comedy called *Mikey and Nicky*.

Falk pulled himself away from the omnipresent pressures of his television series to join Cassavetes and Miss Rowlands at their stately memento-packed home in the Hollywood Hills for this discussion of the ideas and attitudes involved in their new movie. This exclusive *Viva* interview was conducted by Dick Adler.

Viva: John, you've said that none of your stories can be described well in a few sentences. So I think I'll ask Gena what *A Woman Under the Influence* is about.

Gena: Someone asked me that the other day, and I told her the story of the picture. John happened to overhear it, and he said, "What picture are you talking about?" I really have come to the conclusion then that if I were able to tell a story, I wouldn't be an actress.

John: Gena's trying to say that there's very little story. This is basically a story about a man who lets a woman go. The thing that comes to mind is that women get double-crossed all the time in life, and being double-crossed they suffer loneliness, discomfort, envy of a man's job, and a place unrecognized in our society—being a mother and somebody devoted to a husband. What in hell says that a woman has to be under a man's influence? Ideally speaking—and idyllically speaking—a man would *like* a woman to be under his influence, but oftentimes he doesn't want to take the responsibility for that influence. I think that's basically the theme of this picture. It's the story of a woman who's in love with a man, married to him, mother of his three children, and he's in love with her. It's an assumption picture—assuming that a wife is everything a man wants her to be, how could he let her go? It really shows, beyond any other movie I've ever seen, the real, solid differences between men and women.

Viva: John, you once told an interviewer that men were more complicated than women—more complex characters. Doesn't that strike you as a little bit patronizing?

John: Well, women *are* always being accused of changing from day to day, and I think that women change for definite reasons. But I think that men change just because they feel like changing, for no reason at all. Women change because their influences change.

Gena: I was brought up in an unusual situation; my mother was a feminist and my father was a male chauvinist, but they got along marvelously. So nobody even suggested putting me into any pigeonholes when I was growing up. If I said I wanted to be a nurse, it was almost "How dare you not want to be a doctor?" Still, I realized then and realize now that for a woman it has always been an enormous effort to be everything that is expected of you. And that effort can finally become so overwhelming that it's a burden to a man. The slightest rejection on his part can send you into a wild, crazy thing—now I'm speaking as the character in the movie—and it becomes not only a problem for the woman but a *terrible* problem for the man. Now do you see why John doesn't ask me to tell the story of the picture?

John: Well, I really believe that all women are crazy. They've been driven crazy by playing a role they can't fulfill. Of course, all men are crazy, too. Let's face it—we all want to have a good time to begin with; none of us is that bright or godlike. We go out when we're young and we play, and every day has no meaning; it just runs right into the next day. And then suddenly all of us are bound with responsibilities—we're called upon to be adults suddenly. When two strange people, a man and a woman, meet in a one-to-one situation, in order to come together and love they must have everything in common. And if they're a man and a woman, I really contend that society *allows* them nothing in common. That's what the picture is all about.

Viva: Peter, you must get about five hundred movie scripts a year—all the top plums. What was there in this one to make you work for nothing and invest some of your own money in it on top of that?

Peter: I was touched by the character of the woman Gena plays—she was extremely moving to me.

Viva: What about the man, the character of her husband? What attracted you to him?

Peter: He was funny, and that's always good for me. The first time I read him, I laughed out loud. He's funny, though not too aware of what's going on. A dope—not a bad man, but a dope. He's in over his head. He's involved with something he doesn't know how to deal with. He's very much in love with this woman and excited by her—he can have fun with her. But he doesn't quite know how to handle her; she makes demands on him that he can't handle.

Viva: John, I can't think of any other director who is as involved—even obsessed—with the relationships between men and women. Perhaps Eric Rohmer, who did *My Night at Maud's*, in France, but certainly nobody in this country. Why is that? Don't you ever want to go out and direct a cowboy or spy movie?

John: I guess it's just a matter of interest to me that every day we have to live with our image of ourselves as seen by the opposite sex. Everything that affects our lives is determined by the influence that one sex has upon the other. Sure we're in the midst of political decay and turmoil—but that's not nearly as interesting. That's more mental, based on how much information you have. The relationships between men and women are permanently fixed in our instincts, not our minds.

Viva: Peter, what is there about John as a director that makes actors get so deeply involved in his films—makes them pass up more lucrative projects and certain successes to take a chance with him?

Peter: He's not boring.

Viva: What else?

Peter: That's plenty when you start to think about it. You know somebody for three or four years and you're never bored—what else is there? Jesus, you spend your whole life doing other pictures; you did them already and you'll do a million of them before you're dead. You usually go on a picture and everybody is a stranger. Working with people that you know and like—I don't care what you're doing—is a big edge. It takes a long time to reach the point where you have mutual confidence. People can go for years before they reach that point where there's an honest exchange, where you're not worried about petty feelings and egos. I think that all actors and directors have this dream—if there were only ten of us and we could spend the rest of our lives working together, not to have to always move from stranger to stranger.

Viva: What does this kind of mutual admiration society do to your critical judgment of the work at hand? Would you do anything John asked you to?

John: No—only this year Peter turned me down cold on a movie with Elaine May and Gena. It was going to be a comedy set in Las Vegas about some people who liked to dance. Maybe the fact that I was going to be in it changed his mind.

Peter: You can't be an artist if you say yes to everything; if you do, you're not an individual with individual tastes. I think that's what joins us together—that somehow, even if we don't qualify as artists, we're at least artistically inclined.

Viva: Gena, I'm sure that one of the things people must have asked you most often is whether you and John are working out your real problems through your movies. How do you react to that?

Gena: A part of it has to come from our own lives, of course, but I don't think these kinds of problems are any more common to us than to people who aren't actresses or directors. *A Woman Under the Influence* is quite an extreme picture—I mean, the woman is committtably wacko!—and yet every time we show it I hear people saying, "My God! This is the story of my life!" It shocks me to hear them say it, even though I've suspected it for a long time.

No, certainly the movie isn't the story of John's and my life. But I do think that I can in some way represent women in America at this time. I'm a feminist in that I've been a self-supporting woman since I was eighteen years old. I am a wife to a husband; I'm a mother to three children. I am not a cupcake actress—though I have nothing against them, and I don't mean that to sound condescending. My emphasis in life is deeply split between these two things—to be an actress and to be a mother. It's a great conflict in my life.

Okay, being an actress and a mother is an extreme case. But how different is the woman in this movie? She's uneducated, married to a hard-hat guy. She's not complicated, she's never heard of Freud or Jung or Adler. All she feels is this enormous pull—the same one I feel. And it breaks something that she thought could never be broken, in herself and in her marriage.

Viva: John, what are your feelings about suggestions that you often use your films as a catharsis for your own problems?

John: I'll use anything I can to straighten out a problem—even write a movie about it. Look at it this way, if I were writing a picture and I used a situation which none of us were involved in or interested in, then I'd feel ashamed about doing it—and so would everybody else. So I use absolutely everything I can find, in our own lives, in our friends' lives, to make what we're doing interesting.

Viva: For example, there was a perfect little gem of a scene in *Minnie and Moskowitz* in which Gena as Minnie and John as the married man she'd been sleeping with have a tremendous argument. Can you say *that* didn't come out of one of your own battles?

Gena: If we ever divorce, I'm taking that scene to court!

John: I'd say that scene was more of a theatrical adventure than a realistic copy of what happens around here.

Viva: What about you, Peter? Does acting in John's films seem any more connected to your real life than what you do in *Columbo*?

Peter: I don't know if it's any more autobiographical, but working for John is certainly harder than anything else I do. It's much more demanding and complicated. *Columbo* is still fun for me—except for getting the scripts right, which is not fun and never will be. But actually playing it, playing a good scene in *Columbo*—I love it. I even still learn things from it. I think I mug less now than when I first started the show. I think I play it a little less obviously.

But acting in John's pictures is harder than that, and harder than in almost anybody else's pictures, because he establishes a standard of reality or immediacy or spontaneity that is different than in other pictures. In other pictures, you can get away with very fine acting—good, skillful acting—but if you try to put that same kind of acting into one of John's pictures it will stick out like a sore thumb. You know it just won't work. So you have to try to be effective without relying on any of those technical skills which you've acquired over the years, without using all those things which come easy to you. Also, this is a much more complicated script than most stories you get to do—the characters are more complex. You have a night scene with these two people, quite a romantic scene, and then the next day he has to commit her to a mental hospital—that's hard to make work.

Viva: Gena, didn't you ever think it was presumptuous on John's part to write a film like *A Woman Under the Influence*, which is primarily told from the woman's point of view?

Gena: I can't imagine it being presumptuous for a writer to try to get *anything* down on paper! On the other hand, it's presumptuous for a human being even to try to get a *letter* written to another human being! Even that for me is a torture chamber with the screws in the fingernails. . . .

John: It's not presumptuous because I don't feel that women are particularly unique—that's the first thing. The second thing is that I have a definite person in mind when I write—in this case, Gena—which is why I like to work with people who are very close to me. I know the way they think, so I try—*presume*, if you will—to put down some of those thoughts, not in their own terms but in the character's terms.

Gena: That's what makes John's scripts so very different. Most scripts you get, you know in the first five or ten pages exactly what's going to happen, what's expected of you. With John's scripts, it's like being an astronaut on the moon for the first time—the air is very light, you have to wear heavy boots, you have to push yourself out into areas that are very frightening.

I suppose I push further for John than for any other director, but not because he's my husband. When we work together, he *isn't* my husband anymore—he's the enemy and I want to put my hands around his throat and choke him a good deal of the time. I don't push hard for him because he's John and I'd like to please him; it's because he happens to be the kind of artist and director that he is. I know that other actors feel the same way—and they're not even married to him!

Viva: Peter, did you have any idea how *Husbands* would look when it was finished?

And how about *A Woman Under the Influence*—how much like the finished film was your mental picture of it while it was being made?

Peter: On *Husbands* I saw all the dailies and so I had some idea of how it would look, how it would all fall together. The total impact—that I couldn't imagine. On this last one, I didn't know at all what the finished picture would be like. I was surprised—and a little bit frightened. It's a very powerful statement.

Viva: John, ever since your first film, *Shadows*, many people have thought of you as a director who improvises much—if not all—of your films. Would you like to take this opportunity to comment on this?

John: Improvisation to me means that there is a characteristic spontaneity in the work which makes it appear not to have been planned. I write a very tight script, and from there on in I allow the actors to interpret it the way they wish. But once they choose their way, then I'm extremely disciplined—and they must also be extremely disciplined about their own interpretations.

So in that sense it's each person being an individual rather than a team member working for the benefit of the movie—and in that same sense the editing room becomes *my* improvisation. It's my job to retain all the individual characteristics they put into the thing—which is a total impossibility, of course, and explains why I've spent ten years of my life in editing rooms—and also to make the film work as a whole. I'm not saying this is a better way of working than anyone else's. I know it's a much more difficult way, though, and one more prone to failure. But it's more rewarding for the people to work on it, and if we ever hit a big one—as I think we've done with this picture—then the results can be *terrifying*.

Viva: John, every time you finish a film you're full of this enormous enthusiasm for it. How long can you sustain that enthusiasm? Do you go back to your films and see them again and wonder why you were so excited about them? Are they all as wondrous to you now as they were when you'd just finished them?

John: I think the wondrous part about it is not so much the film itself but the working conditions on that film. It's not so much the job that you're on, but the associations you make and the people that you're dealing with—having fun with or suffering with—that makes a film important to you.

To me, *Shadows* will always be the film I love the best—simply because it was the first one and we were all young, and because it was impossible, and we were so ignorant, and for three years we survived each other and everything.

By the time the second one rolls around, you're prepared to make all the mistakes. When the third one comes you try to be good, and by the time the fourth arrives you'd better be ready and have some reason to do it. But you don't really—you're just older, more mature.

My fourth one happened to be *Faces*, which was an elegant, wonderful group of people who got together and worked for six months on a film without any pay—just taking the risk, much like the first one. So I have a soft spot in my heart for *Shadows* and *Faces*.

With *Husbands*, I met two great guys—Peter and Ben Gazzara—and we became very good friends right on the spot. I didn't think that it was possible to make new friendships at forty, but it is. *Minnie and Moskowitz*, as I've said, was a theatrical adventure—a poem about ordinary people.

As for *A Woman Under the Influence*, I think it's the first picture that I've had anything to do with that wasn't made out of plain, simple feeling, but rather out of a real desire to do something in my profession. It was extremely frightening for me not to come to work out of enthusiasm and instead put myself up as something of a craftsman.

The idea was to take all the experiences that I've had, all the family and love that's been given, all the bitterness—you know that as you get older you lose friends as well as make them, you have disappointments and tragedies, they come faster—to take all that and say, "Okay, we've had all this" and put it all together. Of course the idea itself has to be good—it really has to be first-rate.

I think that if there is any fault in *A Woman Under the Influence*, it's that the film is so damned powerful that it deprives the senses of air. We've screened it dozens of times and we've worked on it in the editing room for two years, and I've never once seen it without being shaky.

I've lost sight of what the result of the film will be because I don't *know* what the separation or togetherness of a man and woman mean in this day and age. It leaves some people feeling extremely bitter, it leaves some feeling uplifted. Some think it's funny, others think it's extremely sad. And everybody thinks that Gena and Peter are terrific.

Viva: John, do you see your pictures as some sort of a continuing chain, or do they just happen to be where you are at any particular moment?

John: Both, I think. It *is* a continuous feeling in a way—you start out extremely young and make an extremely young picture. As you get older, you make pictures about the way you feel at the time, and hopefully you can keep that feeling alive. That's what I like about being an actor, writer, director—and about being friends with actors, writers, and directors. We all have come to the realization that we can't be cynical. That's the only way I know that you can really put yourself up and speak for other people—to preserve that innocence so that you're not aware that you have no *right* to speak for other people. Because once you start having that awareness, then it's really time to walk away.

Viva: Where does that innocence end and naïveté—which is one of the other things you've been charged with—begin?

John: Maybe there's no difference. There are certain people in this business—and it really *is* a business—who don't like my work for that very reason, because it's not done in the conventional, cool, cynical way. People have said that my films are very difficult to watch, that they're experiences you are put through rather than ones you enjoy, and it's true. I remember when we made *Shadows* some guy from my hometown said, "John, what kind of a movie is that? It's about me! Who the hell's interested in me?"

Viva: There's another kind of innocence which you seem to be fond of—commercial innocence. Every time you've made a film, you've had to go through the whole complicated process of getting the money together from your friends. Why haven't you ever taken the easier road of getting involved in the financial mainstream?

John: I don't think it's been a deliberate choice. People do what they're capable of doing. If I could take a lot of money from studios and enjoy myself at cocktail parties, I probably would make a conscious effort to take that route. I'm just not capable of doing it. But I don't think it's any great credit—or discredit either—to me that I can't.

Viva: So you don't think that the guys who are making those big, studio-backed blockbusters are in a different business?

John: No. Not for a minute. Anybody who works all day learning words, trying to find a character, can't really get involved in making great separations between what's good and bad. I think you work harder sometimes on crap than you do on something that's not crap. Who knows the difference? The most well-intentioned work can sometimes be just terrible. And even your best friends won't tell you.

The best you can do is try to put down what happens in your own life, the things you can understand and comprehend, and then take a chance with it—say that this is what I'm thinking and feeling now—so let's get some people together who think and feel the same way, and we'll all take our best shot at it.

A Woman Under the Influence:
An Interview with John Cassavetes

Judith McNally / 1975

From *Filmmakers Newsletter* (January 1975): 23–27.

It's hard to find a lukewarm reaction to John Cassavetes's work. Mention the films of this highly original, fiercely independent actor/writer/director and you usually touch off a chorus of superlatives praising his ability to capture day-to-day reality, his emotional truth and intensity, and his innovative filmic techniques. Once in a while, however, a dissenting voice is heard: "Can't stand that man's stuff!" And however ad hominem it may be, you can't help wondering if such a stern negative reaction doesn't grow from the fact that Cassavetes's films can hit home with an accuracy which some are bound to find uncomfortable.

His latest film, *A Woman Under the Influence*, is no exception. On the surface, it's a simple enough story: Mabel Longhetti is a young housewife both supported and smothered by her husband, three small children, and a close-knit, demanding Italian-American family. We see her make the transition from charming kookiness to full-fledged emotional disturbance, both because and in spite of her husband's well-intentioned, fumbling attempts to "straighten her out." As Judith Crist put it, the film brings us "to the very core of a mind in retreat."

Yet Nick and Mabel (brilliantly played by Peter Falk and Gena Rowlands, Cassavetes's wife) are hardly excerpts from a psychiatric textbook. Rather, like all Cassavetes's characters, they are fully conceived, fully realized human beings: no stranger and no smarter than most of us, coping as best they can with universals like marriage, families, pain, and loneliness. As usual, Cassavetes has cast some important supporting roles with nonprofessionals, many of them his friends and relatives, and has drawn such excellent performances from them that, as one top critic phrased it, it almost makes nepotism seem desirable.

Like all his previous films, *A Woman Under the Influence* was independently produced and financed. The facts of his career bear out what you quickly sense in talking with the man: he has the courage of his convictions. He wants to do his films the best way he knows how, and if that means going it alone, well, that's what he does. Risky? Of course. But the risks have paid off. His first film, *Shadows* (shot over three years with his acting students) received critical acclaim and several awards. *Faces* won numerous awards including three Academy Award nominations. *Too Late Blues*, *A Child Is Waiting*, *Husbands*, and *Minnie and Moskowitz*, all of them popularly and critically successful, complete the roster.

Cassavetes was in New York for the premiere of *A Woman Under the Influence* at the NY Film Festival and we were able to talk for several hours. As is usually the case, his stay in town was a tightly scheduled round of press conferences, talk shows, and interviews. In those circumstances, an interview can often become a carefully choreographed ritual as a tired, harried director does his best to hide his fatigue while trotting out pat answers to questions he's already answered a dozen times.

It is not the case when you talk with John Cassavetes. He's intense, volatile, down-to-earth, and unpretentious. And when we got down to what John considers brass tacks: people, working with actors (not surprising, since he was a successful TV and film actor before turning filmmaker), and the film industry—then hot coffee got cold and cigarettes went unlit for unnervingly long periods while he stated his case, by turns vehement, thoughtful, even angry. But always candid. I kept waiting for the almost standard "Of course, this is all off the record," but it never came. It was hardly a typical interview; but then, John Cassavetes is far from a typical filmmaker.

Judith McNally: How did you get involved in doing the screenplay for *A Woman Under the Influence*? Is it something you had wanted to do for a long time?

John Cassavetes: I think we're just reporters, all of us basically. And a story like this is not newsworthy really—it's not Watergate, it's not war; it's a man and woman relationship, which is always interesting to me. And in telling a story, I think the important thing is to make it correspond to the emotions of the audience you're addressing. I have a total awareness that a film can be successful only because an audience is interested in a particular subject. The quality of the film itself doesn't affect an audience as much as the subject you choose.

JM: Did you have a particular audience in mind?

JC: Yes—people. Women and men, to be more specific. Actually, *A Woman Under the Influence* was first a trilogy of three-act plays which I converted to one screenplay. It was hard to cut down, and the finished film is long. As I get older, I guess I have a tendency to make longer pictures. But the subjects are also more difficult. I don't think audiences are satisfied any longer with just touching the surface of people's lives; I think they really want to get into a subject.

JM: I certainly didn't find the length excessive, but two and a half hours is long for a feature. Do you anticipate any trouble from theater owners?

JC: I haven't had any. No one has brought it up. This film deals with the serious problems of a man and woman who are alienated from each other by their backgrounds, ignorant of their problems, yet totally in love. If we rushed the story just to get to the dramatic areas, it would no longer be a valid picture. So I can't take into consideration what some theater owner or distributor might think—I couldn't care less.

JM: How tightly was the film scripted?

JC: I think it's in the modern screenplay tradition—if there is such a thing. The old screenplays, as you know, detailed every shot, every angle, every location. Today we just don't do that; pictures are much more loosely made. This script was really for the actors, so we did have all the dialogue scripted.

JM: One of the hallmarks of your films is the consistently brilliant performances you get from your actors. Do you do a lot of rehearsing?

JC: Not that much. I just use very good actors; that helps! I really believe almost anyone can act. How *well* they can act depends on how free they are and whether the circumstances are such that they can reveal what they feel. I don't think there's any great trick to my directing: I just get people I like, people I'm interested in, and talk to them on the basis of their being people rather than actors.

If an actor wants to do something in a certain way, I don't want to tell him that wouldn't be right—that would be crazy. I'm never aware of anyone being bad; I don't have that type of criticism in me. I believe everything until the actor stops and questions. I don't want big, long discussions; I don't want to know what they're thinking. If an actor tells me, "Look, I'm going to be this" and then tries to do it, he's putting untold pressure on himself.

JM: Can you explain why you often work with both amateurs and professionals in the same picture?

JC: I find it very easy because they help each other. The amateur has no preconceived notions of how it should be done; the professional has: he's gone to school, learned techniques, knows what will work—his choices, his selections, are usually better. The amateur has no selection: it's a very pure thing. So the professional gets a little jealous while the amateur begins to pick up a few things. Somewhere in the course of the film they come together and aid each other: the professional takes purity from the amateur, and the amateur takes on a certain amount of professionalism.

JM: Do you consciously direct this process, or does it just sort of happen by osmosis?

JC: I think it's all in the atmosphere. It's very hard to let the technical processes of film take over and then expect the actors to reveal themselves. I mean, you can't take a shower at a dinner party. If I have any special way of working, it's just to set up an atmosphere where what the actors are doing is really important, fun, and nothing takes precedence over it.

For that reason, the choice of the crew becomes extremely important. They have to understand that what they're doing—no matter how hard they're working—is only to help what's going on in front of the camera. Audiences are not watching the technical processes as hard as they're watching the actors. If the actors are good, the picture looks good—I mean, the actual photography looks better when the actors are better.

On a set there's really a lot that can hamper the actors. For example, in this film, here's maybe the most important moment in two people's lives: a guy is committing his wife to a mental hospital. But someone is also fiddling with your hair, putting lipstick on you, placing lights above you, sitting you down, marking your feet, moving cameras, yelling, "Hey, she doesn't look good; her skin is out of focus." Now, I ask you, how can the actors concentrate? So we do all this *before* the actors come onstage. We all work quietly, and hopefully efficiently, and get it done.

JM: In this film the performance of the three small children is critically important at times. Did you find any special problem in working with such young children?

JC: It is different. You're always stooping to the children, always aware they are children. You don't quite know how much they can comprehend or how good they're going to be, so you're always terribly afraid they're going to be little snot-nosed cute kids.

I found the best approach was to be kind of cold to the kids, not to deal with them as children and not to worry whether they'd do well. I just hoped they would pick up, as an adult would, where the story was going. As a matter of fact, I was really quite thrilled. At the end of the picture, there's a scene where Peter Falk is apparently attacking his wife, and the kids *automatically* attacked the father. I never said for them to do that, they just did it—and in an exquisite way. The delicacy with which they approached their own intervention and the taking of sides was something that could never have been *told* to them. You just try not to put any pressure on the children so they can listen and do things their own way. And I think they did.

Now in working with the kids, or any actors for that matter, I certainly give directions—but I'm not aware of it. And hopefully, the people I give them to are not aware of taking them. So I know, for example, they went up the stairs and I must have said something about it, but I tried to do it within the framework of the action so it didn't become a set direction. I might have said, "Take them up the stairs, Pete," and then eliminated that from the soundtrack.

JM: One striking thing about your films is your use of the camera to select, probe, and reveal. How closely do you work with the cinematographer in planning camera moves and angles?

JC: Obviously, you have to begin by putting the camera somewhere. But I feel there is no such thing as setting up a shot that is "right" for the scene. So I'm left just shooting the action, and the selections are those of the operator. If the operator is free to think in those terms, he can simply photograph what's happening without constricting the actors.

Usually the actors don't know what's being shot. Even though we sometimes shoot very tight, they never know when the camera's going to swing onto them, so everyone has to play every moment. If you set up a formalized shot, the tendency is for the actors to let down when they're not on screen. So the fluidity of the camera really keeps it alive and allows the operator to make his selections emotionally.

JM: In that long sequence when Mabel is committed, it was fascinating the way people kept going in and out of focus and it very much matched the emotional dynamics of the scene. Was that carefully pre-planned?

JC: We just set it up on such an extremely long lens that I knew it would be technically impossible to do it all in focus. The operator and the focus puller couldn't possibly be in concert because there'd be no way of knowing where the actors would be at any moment. It had to be a natural thing: certain things would come in and out of focus because there were so many points of interest switching back and forth all the time.

We did that sequence many different times in many different ways. But out of maybe twelve takes, this was the only one that seemed to play in continuity in terms of performances and everything else.

JM: And it was all shot in one long take?

JC: Oh, yes. I shoot almost everything in ten-minute takes—unless, of course, it's a very short scene. I'm not bright enough (and I don't think anyone is really) to get everything all at once. If there are emotions and revelations taking place a mile a minute, how can we separate all these things with our camera and then go into an editing room and try to make selections? It would be really impossible.

I have to get a take that plays. If we don't see Peter for a moment, or if we don't see Gena for a moment, it's not that important. The important thing is to play whatever action is most interesting at the moment. I'm not going to stand over the camera operator's shoulder and say, "Swing over to that. . . . Do you have a good frame there?" It's more like documentary work. Besides, we had a wonderful camera crew. I knew they would be as artistic as possible and would frame in such a way that it wouldn't seem like a movie.

JM: Did you do a lot of handheld shooting in this film?

JC: Twenty-five percent or 30 percent of the film was handheld. And I do all the handheld shooting myself. I like to use it where it wouldn't ordinarily be used— for example in an acting scene rather than in an action sequence—for fluidity, for intensity.

Besides, once there's a handheld camera up there, the actors go much faster. When I'm shooting, I think nothing of saying to the actors: "Get the hell out of there, move, move!!"—but I don't think the camera operators would dare to take that privilege.

JM: About how many takes did you usually do per scene?

JC: It depended on the difficulty of the writing. If the writing was excellent, the scenes went easily. If the writing wasn't too good and there were loose or open ends, then we did several takes, sometimes up to twelve or fourteen.

I shoot a *lot* of film because I shoot ten-minute takes. I can't stand to have an actor go through a whole scene in master and then simply because he has nothing to do shift him into one little thing: "Now look here . . . Look there . . . Fine. Cut. Print." I'd rather spend a little bit more time and money and give the actor an opportunity to play the scene with other actors who are also playing the same scene. So our ratio goes up. We had a thirteen-week shooting schedule and must have shot 600,000 or 700,000 feet of film. The finished film is about 13,000 or 14,000 feet.

JM: Did you do much multiple-camera work here?

JC: Not too much. We were shooting in regular 35mm with a Mitchell BNC. We used an Arri for a second camera—for the handheld work and for exteriors. Mainly we used long lenses and wide angles. We tried to match their look by setting the optics so we'd always be shooting from underneath, which gives the wide angle the same appearance as the long lens.

One of the reasons we used long lenses, especially for all the work in the house, was to avoid a feeling of confinement. So much of the picture takes place in the Longhetti house there's a real danger of getting the feeling the actors are locked in by the camera. The long lenses meant the camera could be far away and the actors wouldn't be constricted by its proximity. And after a while, the actors weren't aware of the camera. It seemed to work very well, very easily.

The location could have been a serious problem. At first everyone said, "How can you do a picture where 80 percent of it happens in the same house?" I think that's one reason why we had such difficulty financing the picture; it didn't seem to have enough movement, enough openness. But we decided we wouldn't try to exploit the house or make a "thing" of it. So most of it was shot in the dining room and the foyer, basically from two angles. One good thing about the house, of course, was that we could shoot all the sequences there in continuity.

JM: Was it hard to find a house like that with that extremely big, open entrance hall?

JC: We looked at maybe 150 houses in Los Angeles. It was really hard to find something in the right price range that would make you feel you were in a real house and also depict the kind of blue-collar existence we had in mind. Some of the houses we scouted had plastic covers on everything, plastic pictures on the walls, and most of the family's money went into electrical appliances. That's a very real thing, but we didn't want it. So we decided we needed a hand-me-down house and finally found one that had been given to the Nick character and still had all the old furniture and old woodwork.

We had an incredibly talented art director, Phedon Papamichael, who has worked with us before. Not only was he the art director, he was the whole fun of the production. His desire to keep that house neat and clean (and it was an important part of Mabel's character that she was a good housekeeper) was fanatic; he had his cleaning fluid out all the time. He'd say: "I don't want anyone walking in the set"—and this with thirty or forty people around! Or, "If anyone smokes, I kill them! I kill them with my hands! I throw them down on the ground and kill them!" He really kept everything quite alive.

JM: What was the budget?

JC: We didn't *have* a budget. We got as much as we could free: food and Coca-Cola and beer and whatever we could grub. I haven't even gone over the budget yet, but I imagine it's somewhere in the vicinity of $800,000.

JM: Faces International Films, the production company, is your company, isn't it?

JC: Yes. Peter Falk and I did the financing. We went into this together and he deferred his salary. He loved the picture; he's a great actor and very artistically oriented. He is also about the best friend I have in the world.

JM: What directors do you feel have influenced your work?

JC: Well, I'd like to feel that people have influenced me, but then when you get on the floor you realize you're really alone and no one can influence your work. They can just open you up and give you confidence that the aim for quality is really the greatest power a director can have—if you're in quest of power. In a way, you must be out for power. We wouldn't make films if we didn't think that in some way we could speak for everyone.

When I was a kid, Frank Capra was certainly America to me. In terms of today's directors I think Marty Scorsese is phenomenal and singular. I very much like Don Siegel for what he does, and Bob Altman for what he does, and also Bogdanovich, Melvin van Peebles, Aldrich, Shirley Clarke, Antonioni, Lumet, and certainly Elaine May. In a way I admire them all: each picture is different, every person has a different strength. When it comes right down to it, I admire anyone who can make a film.

JM: Sooner or later the question comes up of whether film is an art or a craft.

JC: I think film is magic. With the tools we have at hand, we really try to convert people's lives.

Directors are alone because their work is so disproportionate to daily life. When you become a director, you take on the responsibility not just of making a picture and putting yourself on the line as a person, but you're also saying: "Today I am going to make a great movie. I am also going to be successful. I am going to reach an audience so I can make my next film." I hate the present system of directing because there's too much pressure to be good. There's no relaxation at all. You're constantly aware of the financial responsibility, the fact that your life without directing is very empty, and that you have to make a successful movie. So your instincts and what you know sometimes give way to what you have to do. You must please distributors and your audience.

I see people like Bob Altman, Elaine May, Elia Kazan—great directors. These people shouldn't be left alone. Somewhere along the line there has to be somebody who makes things easier. Not someone who says (like most distributors) "Can you do it? Can you be a killer? Can you pretend that everything is right?"

I think the greatest thing a director can do is keep himself straight, realize that he or she doesn't have to know all the answers and be content with enjoying oneself without thinking about what's going to happen afterwards. That's very hard to do. You have to be somewhat innocent.

JM: You've always stayed well away from the usual Hollywood system. Do you think it's possible to maintain that kind of innocence in it?

JC: I don't think I could ever make another film like this again. And I'm not talking about the quality of the film—I mean the kind of film where you do everything. I've done it four times, and I don't know that I could do it again. I would want to have more ease and relaxation; I would want to have some endorsement of my talent and the film I'm making.

This way, it's too difficult. You say to yourself, well, what is it? It's a film. All right, it affects people's lives. Maybe it'll connect with somebody. But it doesn't affect *my* life that much—I'm just putting down what I know. So is it worth it to kill yourself to make the film and bring it to an audience so that someone will applaud? Or so that you'll have a big house? I can't like making films anymore if they're this tough. The pressures are too unnatural. I'm not crying, because I enjoy it. But I am saddened by the fact that I have physical limitations.

At the end of every film you have to say goodbye to everybody. Here are people who worked night and day and killed themselves and at the end you shake hands and go away and now all of a sudden all the credit belongs to me! And to the actors who put in their thirteen weeks—while other people put two years into it. At the end, I feel this bitterness and hostility because I've got to walk away and do another film that may not have anything to do with them. It seems like a double-cross.

If a major distributor comes in, the people who made the film possible are not acknowledged—they're not even given a ticket to see the movie! That's a big reason against major distributors.

We're distributing *A Woman Under the Influence* ourselves because the studios have had no interest in it. And if they did come to us, we wouldn't sell it cheaply because we've taken our risks and expect to be paid well for it. After all, who the hell are they? Unless they finance the production, they're a bunch of agents who go out and book theaters; that's what it really boils down to. Sure, being a distributor is a craft in itself, and if they had done a better job we'd all be in better condition. They've lost millions and millions of dollars because of their petty egos. Most of them don't have any real interest in films. How could they? They hate artists anyway.

Everyone who makes a film is at the major distributors' mercy. We don't want great sums of money, but we do expect distributors to offer us some continuity and be more practical: not to offer actors a million dollars when times are good and make the business impossible; not to take 25 percent overhead so they can put more money in their coffers; and not to make destructive pictures they don't even believe in. They'd make a picture about a revolution in which all major studio heads were killed if they thought it would make money.

That's the kind of impossible situation that makes paranoids out of all people who make films. We have to contend with it; we accept it, and in accepting it we hurt ourselves and everyone else around us. I don't say I've been a saint in my life, but I couldn't sell my soul out for things I just don't believe in. And if that means I'll never make film again, then I'll never make another film again.

JM: You don't have any plans at all for another film?

JC: Right now all I can hope is that the picture is extremely successful. And if it isn't, I won't make another one—that's all. Which in itself is no great tragedy.

The real tragedy is that other poor young filmmakers are coming along who will go out and conform before they've ever opened their mouths. Occasionally you'll get a Marty Scorsese who has a kind of independence built into his body that enables him to withstand it. But he'll be abused because he's independent. These idiots don't realize that to be independent isn't something *against them*, it's something *for good films*. And they'll never understand that as long as they're lawyers, as long as they're accountants, as long as the deal is more important than the movie itself. As long as this exists, they will have difficulty making money.

And yet it *is* an art, a beautiful art. It's a madness that overcomes all of us; we're in love with it. Money is really not that important to us; we can work thirty-six, forty-eight hours straight and feel elated at the end of that time. It's incredibly hard—but if you have bitterness connected with it, it's impossible.

The one difference between the film industry now and the old days is that back then nobody had responsibility to make a *great* film. They had a responsibility to sucker in the big guys, band together, and have fun on their own small level. Through that, the accidents of great films occurred because the love was always there. All those guys had pride in making a good film, if only to be able to say, "Well, our picture was good at least." No one thought in terms of millions of dollars.

Now the big question is: can a picture make $100 million? Who the hell cares? If you're thinking that way, you're not making films, you're making money. If that's what it's come to, let the audience look at pictures of money, put money on the screen, and then rape it, shoot it, defecate on it—because that's basically what everyone is doing.

I'm not really an angry person, but I get angry when I see people of extraordinary talent and ability abused so terribly by the majors who defile anything. That's why I admire Sidney Lumet: because I think he's been able to withstand those pressures somehow.

I don't understand why people in our business are such hypocrites. We never sit around discussing how much money a picture is going to make, we discuss the *picture*, whether it's good or bad. I don't mind criticism on my films—yes, they *are* long; sometimes I'm not as good as I could be; I may not tell the story as well as I might; maybe I'm clumsy in certain areas. That kind of criticism is terrific.

JM: Do you feel your films have been an evolutionary process? That you learned something in each which you could apply to the next?

JC: Oh, yes. I learned to be more worried about every picture I do, to be more skeptical, to look at people I'm working with and know that I'm using them because there's no ultimate payoff for them, no continuity. That's what I learned. And I also learned to try to keep a story in mind, and to keep people, kindness, and love in mind. You need that to work with people, and it becomes increasingly difficult not only for me but for everyone who works in this stupid business.

I sometimes think we should all go on strike until people become nicer. I can think of one actress, very famous in her day, who is now getting older. She devoted her life to acting and gave people enormous pleasure—but now she's got to look for jobs and is having a hard time of it. What the hell kind of business is that? How can we fail to take care of our own people that way? I see the same people who won't give her work going out and fighting for charities, hospitals, political causes, minorities—but they don't know how to be decent people. If you're successful they say to you: "You're part of a family." They play a shell game; they'll give a guy everything in the world—a big house, millions of dollars—until the minute he fails. Then they don't know him anymore. People live a killer existence, and I don't know how they do it.

JM: What advice would you have for young filmmakers?

JC: I don't know, except they've got to go out by themselves and make films. Hopefully they can make the second film as well as the first. If you go out to make an exploitation film, you're in a lot of trouble today, tomorrow, on your tenth picture. I've never seen a first film by an experimental filmmaker that wasn't good. Never. Not one. I'd love to see everyone's first film: Ford, Capra, Kubrick, Godard, Bergman, and all the others. It would be much more interesting to me to see their first and last films than all those middle successful movies which achieved a certain popularity but weren't necessarily made with the same intent as that first film.

The only thing young filmmakers can do is get some money and make films—any way they can do it. There's no rule. Just get together with good, decent, artistic people and value them—because they're the only ones who will help you.

John Cassavetes, *A Woman Under the Influence*

Larry Gross / 1975

From *Millimeter* (March 1975): 26–31. Reprinted by permission of Larry Gross.

It is fairly early in the morning for John Cassavetes to be giving an interview and the journalist who is talking to him has a questioning voice marred by an unfaked head-cold. Thirty minutes is the tentatively agreed-upon length granted for the discussion. But, lo and behold, after some rough starts and stops at the beginning of the conversation, the two of them go on chatting for an hour and a half. Cassavetes, who made *Too Late Blues* and *A Child Is Waiting* for the studios, and *Shadows, Faces, Minnie and Moskowitz, Husbands*, and *A Woman Under the Influence* as an independent writer-director, has a lot of different things on his mind:

Millimeter: How did you get started on your first feature, *Shadows*?

John Cassavetes: It came out of an acting workshop. It began almost accidentally, out of a desire to accomplish some real creative work out of that workshop situation. Film had always been very attractive to me, from the time I was a kid going to the movies. We wanted to commit a lot of our feelings to a series of locked-in images. And we wanted to change people's lives.

MM: It's pretty hard to see the film. Is there a print around?

JC: Well, the Museum of Modern Art owns a print, and were going to release a print sometime next year. It's coming back to us so we'll see what happens.

MM: One interesting fact that links your last three independent films (*Faces, Husbands, A Woman* . . .) is that you emphasize family life, the fact that your major characters have parents and children, and in-laws. This is fairly rare in Hollywood movies where usually the characters seem to have little family life. Why is this the case?

JC: It's not deliberate, in the original intention. I mean I know that the subject is going to be a family. But I don't know what my initial motivations are. You're interested in where you're going.

MM: And you, personally, are involved that closely with your immediate family?
JC: (laughs) No, why would I say that? I simply mean that one follows one's heart's desire. Most people in movies feel that their activity is so demanding and time consuming that they have to transfer their feelings from what they once loved to something new. Many times women have left their men or men have left their women who were involved in directing films or acting in them. It becomes obsessive, the feeling that there is no room for mothers or fathers unless feelings can be made to correspond to your work. Which they happen to do in my case.

MM: Why?
JC: I guess I'm just a really nice guy, that's all.

MM: In *Faces* and *Husbands*, you dealt with people who were basically middle- and upper-middle class and their problems. In *A Woman Under the Influence* you deal with a group of people who are poorer, less sophisticated. Did you feel you'd said all you wanted to say about the middle class? Were you deliberately drawn to a working-class environment?
JC: Yes. (laughter) That's kind of a crazy question . . . was it intentional? (more laughter) I don't do anything that's hidden in my films. Nothing elite or fashionable or subtle in this kind of choice. Other people worry about classes. I didn't really worry about that. I wanted to make a film about a man and a woman. I wanted to reach the problem faster. This woman has three children. I want her to take care of them herself; I don't want her to have maids and nannies and helpers and all that sort of stuff. I want her to be close to those children and close to her husband and yet alone. It's very hard to be alone if you're in a certain economic class; working-class people understand home and family. It would really be terrible if a woman was separated from that in her own life and in her own mind, and had nothing but that, doing everything for that man and her kids. But it's not only a problem for people who work with their hands and their families. It's also a problem for Park Avenue people. Anyway, I don't deal with a social structure to "expose" it.

MM: You've been quoted as saying that this film, *A Woman Under the Influence*, is your most "optimistic" film to date. Could you explain that?
JC: No, I couldn't. You have to see the film.

MM: Is it because you have some kind of reconciliation at the end?

JC: (laugh, followed by sigh) If that's what you got out of it. I can't sit down and explain what I worked on for two and a half years to you or anyone else in one sentence. I thought it was an optimistic film in my terms. If you see it as not being that, that's an opinion. If you're talking about it being because they get together at the end, that's really a putdown to me.

An interruption: When Cassavetes gives his laugh, the journalist gets a little nervous. The laugh is a mixture of a number of things: a groan, a sigh, a curse, and, well, a laugh. The point is that this particular man is perfectly ready to tell the journalist that he believes a certain question is stupid. It might also be added that deliberately stupid questions sometimes are necessary to provoke a reaction. Suffice it to say that when he wants it to be, Cassavetes's manner is a little unnerving. You would not want John Cassavetes for an enemy if you could avoid it. Conversely, of course, you would feel very safe if you knew he was your friend. Because, when he goes on to speak of those he cares for: Gena Rowlands, Peter Falk, Elaine May, Don Siegel, among others, the tone approaches just the right blend of familiarity and awe, charged with genuine respect. You would like someone to discuss you and your work in that tone of voice.

JC: I get hot. I resent the idea that someone says about the film, "If only the dialogue had been more concise . . . if only the dialogue could have reached some conclusion." Some critic said that and I laughed when I looked at it, because I feel those kinds of scenes are very corny and boring to watch when the words are right on the nose and they're no fun for an actor to play. People talk about improvisation as if I say, "Everybody do what they want," and I take a camera and a movie comes out. It doesn't work that way. Anybody who knows anything about film knows that's crazy. Unless you're shooting a war maybe . . . and even there you have to look for action. There are no accidents in this sense of the specific. A camera breaking down . . . a location not available . . . me being broke . . . these are accidents. You stay up all night long and worry a film to death. To make the assumption that things just happen like that is amazing to me. It doesn't happen that way with actors.

MM: Would you discuss one moment in *A Woman Under the Influence* where the character of Mabel asks her father to "stand up for her" and he thinks she means it literally. I sort of thought of that moment as the key to all the human problems in the film.

JC: Yeah. Well, it's a simple thing. A woman says, "Stand up for me," and the man stands up and at this point the woman doesn't need that. It's a case of tuning into the literal mind of the audience for one moment. You have to give yourself those assurances as well as the audience. You are sure for one fleeting moment of something . . . the entire film is brought together for me in the argument scene near the beginning after the men leave. To me, it's two people trying to really talk to each other on such a specific level: they're two people who are unmistakably in love with one another, they're not covered and they're not supposedly "doing" something for one another . . . in our screwed-up psyches that have been warped all over by thousands of books and millions of feet of tapes and advice from in-laws and relatives and lovers and friends, we don't know how to have one-on-one relationships anymore. That's what that scene is. They're just one-on-one trying to work things out . . . there are few women who don't have some close woman friend to advise them on every step of their relationship and there are no men who do not go out and seek help by drinking in a bar or some other way of proving that they're men. And then both go back and try and have that relationship. It's a lovely thing if you can just love a woman purely or if a woman could love you purely. I thought we had accomplished that in this picture. Gena and Peter with all their problems, and they have a *million*, were more comfortable with each other than they were with anyone else. And when they were alone I don't know if there were two people who liked and respected each other more than any two people I've ever seen. And when something else came in-between them, society, embarrassment, his relatives, his men, his feeling that he is doing the right thing, all of this background, all this doesn't work for the character of Mabel because she is different, she only loves him purely. He has two selves and she only has one . . . (laughs) I don't know if all that means anything.

MM: It does . . . some people have compared this film with Bergman's *Scenes from a Marriage*. Did you like the film? Is this comparison correct?
JC: They're both about men and women, but I don't think the narrative is anywhere near the same. I'm not a critic . . . of course I liked it . . . but I like every film. In every film there are always scenes that have something for me. It's a magical thing we're drawn to. A film always is a reflection of the way people feel at a given time. No matter what kind of artist is making a film, somewhere you can find someone in it who is really representative of his time. Since we're all social animals we're all involved in it. I get excited when I see that other people are thinking and feeling the same things I am and that life is not a complete and total chance.

MM: You directed yourself along with Peter Falk and Ben Gazzara in *Husbands*. Was that a particularly difficult experience?
JC: No, I think Ben and Peter were terrific and I'm proud of the picture.

MM: Was there a problem getting detached from your role in order to direct?
JC: Not in this case. There was a lot of preparation that went into *Husbands*. Ben

and Peter were strangers to me at that point and it was a long conditioning process getting to know and trust and like each other. In terms of technical difficulty, that was a matter of difficult technical conditions which no one really is very good at, because there are so many varying factors. It's hard to become subjective with total belief as an actor must be.

MM: Can you discuss the decision to structure *A Woman Under the Influence* around Gena Rowlands? Did you look at her one day and decide that she and the part were right for each other?

JC: I looked a whole lifetime. What I look at when I see Gena is a tremendous actress. I find it difficult in terms of work to look at any other woman and see what I see in this woman. She's an incredible instrument. She has incredible excitement and she's exposed and she has all the attributes of being a great actress . . . When we were doing this I was always thinking of a character as involving you in some kind of human problem that had to be faced. When this film was being written there were some things in the air: the plight of women, the plight of love vs. the home. I thought that was the important problem and Gena thought so too. We didn't have to discuss that, we knew it: that love created at once an atmosphere for living and great moments of beauty and that on the other hand it makes you a prisoner. This is complicated in turn by other characters and their lifestyles that come and go within the structure of the film. The interrelations between the characters must not be made too easy, like people in life each presents unique problems, so that even though they come from the same class background and share similar experiences, problems still arise. Usually we put film in such simple terms while being endlessly involved in talking about our personal experience. We admit how complex it is. But it's as though we never look into a mirror and see what we are. So the films I make really are trying to mirror that emotion, so we can understand what our impulses are . . . why we do things that get us into trouble, when to worry about it, when to let them go. And maybe we can find something in ourselves that is worthwhile . . . Gena put so much of herself into the film that as the picture went along the problems became more and more hers. By the time the picture was over she had so thoroughly understood the investigation that she had made that she had become thoroughly proficient in those aspects of life. She became like Mabel in a sense, *after* the picture was done. Sometimes, you have to snap your fingers and say, "No, no, you're not Mabel; you don't have to get excited every time you see that problem." That's been, uh . . . covered . . . (laughter). It's up to the people in the audience to see it now. If they don't, they won't like your work; they won't like mine. But if they do, it's the ultimate reward.

MM: Have you ever felt an interest in working in some more conventional genre like westerns or gangster films?

JC: Yeah, I did; I started out on the beach when I was ten playing gangster movies as a matter of fact. Most little boys play cops and robbers or cowboys and Indians. But I guess your imagination teaches you that things aren't so simple. When you learn that, you stretch away from the simple idea of make-believe and you try to incorporate those simpler ideas into more complex feelings. I think gangster films are important. I would like to make one, but I would have to make it sheer entertainment . . . That's what we expect from that specific genre, which is a specific American art form . . . My films to my way of thinking are also an art form. I don't know whether I'm capable of making sheer entertainment, but I love it. I'd like to take a comedy and make it tragic.

MM: It's said this has been the best year at the box office in a number of years. Does this affect you, make you optimistic?

JC: I don't want to be a hypocrite and pretend that I really care who else makes money on a film. We have a great deal of difficulty like anyone else, like Altman or Siegel, really, or Scorsese. That never changed whether the industry was doing well or not well; the degree of difficulty is always there.

MM: There's a famous still of you handholding a camera and shooting a scene. How much of your films did you shoot yourself?

JC: Almost everyone on *Faces* shot. George Sims ended up being the main operator because he could handle the Eclair and the conditions that prevailed better than anyone else. Other times Al Ruban, who was the associate producer on *Faces*, shot, because he is the greatest steady man on a straight line. We called [him] "the Truck." If you have to have a dolly that's hand held, there's no one that can move more smoothly than Al Ruban. George has such a tremendous contained energy and physical strength and great sensitivity to what he's shooting. I shot some. [Maurice] McEndree who was the producer shot some. I guess between the four of us we all did a significant amount of work, but it was overwhelmingly Sims's camera head. On *A Woman Under the Influence* I did all the hand-held stuff, except when there were multiple cameras. But I didn't do any of the Mitchell stuff.

MM: What dictates your decision to shoot material yourself?

JC: On hand-held shooting the feeling you want can't be transmitted to a cameraman. It's too delicate. It's not that they don't understand, but I have an enormous advantage in that I'm not afraid to talk to the actors, and you want to be specific at times. I like the hand-held camera, because the actors go faster. In the Mitchell scenes they can be more relaxed. They're not pushed by the camera. A hand-held camera pushes the actor's tempo up without words. In shooting parts of *Faces*, I had this terrible habit of speaking over the soundtrack, almost like being a movie audience. I had so much total faith in what John Marley was doing in that scene where he discovers he's been cuckolded. Marley sees his own youth running away when he makes this discovery. It struck everyone as funny. The sudden realization that you are a fool; it's terrible for yourself, but awfully amusing for other people. So John Marley was standing there, and I kept saying, "Don't look at her, don't look at her, don't look at her," and finally Marley yells, "For Chrissake, John, you blew the whole goddam thing; I can't think when you're talking constantly in a stream." And I hadn't been aware that I was speaking, and then everybody jumped on me and told me that I'd been talking all through the picture. (laughs) They had wished I'd shut up.

MM: Are you quieter now?
JC: Yeah, much more. I learned that discipline, because later on I paid in the editing when I had to clean up crap I'd put on the soundtrack. Although I still do it once in a while.

MM: How do you feel now about your own career as an actor?
JC: Acting is the experience with fellow actors and a script and the director who helps you interpret a role. With Elaine May perhaps, it's been closest to the intention of having the character be full. I just finished working with Peter on her film *Mikey and Nicky*.

MM: I was wondering how you got along with Roman Polanski on *Rosemary's Baby*?
JC: I enjoyed it very much. Not the personal part but the working part. He's an exceptionally talented man, and I worked in areas I hadn't seen before. He was very particular but still all the time creative. He will go through many takes to get what he wants, photographically and emotionally. He's intelligent, and he would shoot many takes of someone just picking up a telephone and he would always come up with new motivations very quickly for new takes . . . an exceptional director. He had a great sense of humor and a sense of intrigue. You're aware of his skill and aware that he knows what he's doing. It's better than working with a dope.

MM: For better or worse you have a reputation as one who makes films that are opposed in conception to films generally financed by the studios. How do you feel about this?

JC: I don't know; proud, I guess. Obviously I'm proud of my work or else I wouldn't do it. But I respect the work of others. I'm obviously not as involved in others' work as I am with my own, but I don't have any general feelings on this. I worked with Elaine for a year or more and that was great. Every situation with every director is different. Lumet has great enthusiasm; Frankenheimer is an exciting guy, always finger snapping. Aldrich was great. He enjoys it when the actor is enjoying himself. That's a wonderful attitude to work under. I'd rather be liked than understood any time. Other guys who direct are more concerned with the front office than they are with the film.

A Conversation with John Cassavetes

Columbia College Chicago / 1975

Previously published by Columbia College, 1975. Reprinted by permission of Columbia College Chicago Archives & Special Collections.

On the evening of March 5, John Cassavetes spoke with the students of Columbia College. Mr. Cassavetes was in Chicago for the opening of his new movie, *A Woman Under the Influence*. Previously, Frank Capra and King Vidor visited Columbia College, but a record of their remarks was not published. This discussion with Mr. Cassavetes was moderated by Anthony Loeb, chairman, film department.

Anthony Loeb: Mr. Cassavetes, Columbia College is a school of the arts and there are people in this room from many disciplines—television, photography, dance, as well as film. This turnout is really a tribute to the vitality of your work.

To our audience, in introducing Mr. Cassavetes, I would like to say that this man is important to me because he works against the grain of Hollywood, not only independent of the studio structure, but also with an individual rhythm, a unique editing style. He works as Bergman works, with his own repertory company . . . his wife, his children, his mother-in-law. His is a highly fruitful nepotism. Let's welcome Mr. John Cassavetes.

John Cassavetes: Thank you. I wish I were taller so I could see everyone. I started a long time ago. I was an actor first, for about five minutes, and then I was an assistant stage manager. One time I was in the back of a theater fooling around and Sam Shaw, who produced *A Woman Under the Influence*, came up to me and asked, "What are you doing now?" I told him and he said, "Well, I'll produce a feature picture if you write it." It was just like that. So I said, "What could I write about? I've never written anything." And he said, "I know a great writer living in Duxbury, Massachusetts. His name is Edward McSorley. If you drive up there and see him, he'll write it with you. But you've got to put an outline of all your ideas on paper, and write about what you know." So I started writing and came back to Sam and he said, "Wonderful! Go up and see McSorley." I said, "I can't. I don't know where he is." He said, "I'll give you his address. I already called him and told him you were coming." I was making eighty-five dollars a week working in a Broadway show as assistant stage manager and I borrowed a friend's car. It was a rumble-seat car and I drove up in the snow and rain without enough gas to get there. I had to borrow money from a cop. Finally I got to this rose-covered cottage in the middle of winter and I thought that was a good sign, that the roses were blooming in winter. I knocked on the door and a guy answered the door. He was a craggy-faced, fifty-five-year-old short prune who looked like a writer is supposed to look. Somebody who's lived a lot, you know. "Hello," he said. "What do you want?" I said, "I'm John Cassavetes. Sam Shaw told . . . you're expecting me, aren't you? I have this manuscript here." He said, "I haven't seen Sam in ten years." Anyway, he invited me in and fed me. His wife was Italian and she fed me bean soup and onions and it was freezing cold and it was terrific. We became good friends, and those are the events surrounding my meeting with Sam Shaw. Our relationship has continued for the past, I don't know, twenty years. Sam introduced me to a lot of things I wasn't aware of—art, music, sculpture, painting. And when you see the films that I make I know you wonder, "What has this man learned?"

Question: How do you feel when you look back at your films? How do they seem to you?

Cassavetes: Well, a film recalls the memory of doing, working with people you like, people with whom you can come into contact on a real level. The kind of people I work with . . . we can fight or scream and yell at each other and still be friends. We can really hate each other with all our hearts and the next day be together because we're working toward a common end. If the film isn't any good, well . . . I just care that we've done the best we can, you know.

Question: Regarding A *Woman Under the Influence*, now that it is playing to audiences, do you see any weaknesses that you didn't perceive before?

Cassavetes: No. I feel that whatever film you make, it's part of your life at a time in your life. To go back and look at it and second-guess it doesn't mean anything, because we did spend two and a half years working on it, you know. Obviously, it was the best we could do. There is a certain desire to making a film, when you really put it in and put it up and you know no limit and you're really willing to die for the film you're making. Now that sounds crazy. If you die for your country, it's not so good, but in film if it's the last thing you ever do, you want your picture to be done. With that attitude, making it that way, a man moves through life really using himself, really making something of his life.

There's a guy named Tim Carey. I don't know whether you've heard of him. He's an actor who was in *Paths of Glory*. He played one of the guys who was executed. He's been in a lot of pictures. Maybe he has an average gross income of, say, three thousand dollars a year over the last twenty-five years. He's been making a picture called *The Little Old Ladies of Pasadena*. He knocks on doors and he says to these old women, "I'm making a film called *The Little Old Ladies of Pasadena* and you're going to come out and get on roller skates with me." And he finds a factory and he goes over to this factory owner and he says, "You're in terrible trouble. I'm the Mafia." And he gets all the roller skates he needs. He has been working on this film about eight years now. There's a trade paper out in California called *Variety*. And Tim makes an announcement every week for seven years that he's just started production. He has no money but he won't give up. He's had a crew of seven hundred people over these eight years. He calls up colleges for help. He convinces people. This man lives for his work. He's what it is all about.

Question: When is he going to know when to stop? When is he going to know when he has enough footage?
Cassavetes: He probably doesn't want to stop, because when he stops then, he really is going to stop, you know. When he stops he'll face the bills that he has to pay. When he stops he'll have to become a father again of seven children. When he stops he'll have to pay attention to his wife. When he stops he'll have to be a human being and to be an artist really is to be a freak, in the greatest sense of the word. You're not interested in living but you're interested in a substitute life, which is what it means to be an artist. Now, not everybody here is going to be an artist and not everybody here is interested in art. Some people are interested in careers and the values that those careers can get them. But if you take some directors, Altman, say. I was his next door neighbor. We were both on the "gimme" when we were working for Screen Gems. We had offices next door to each other. He got signed there and we both were desperately broke. We were both dying because we both wanted to make something and were very unhappy picking up a lot of money doing nothing. He had, at that time, a screenplay he wanted to do, and a staff of people who were really with him. Altman is a good example of what I mean. He is one of the four really independent people in our business.

Question: Who else is in that category?
Cassavetes: Martin Scorsese, Elaine May, Shirley Clarke. It's hard to explain what "independence" means—but to those who have it, film is still a mystery, not a way out. There are other independents, of course, but they haven't really hit the limelight yet, so not enough is at stake. To still do what you want after ten years, twenty years, is something. I've known a lot of filmmakers who started out with enormous talents and lost momentum. I don't say they're selling out, but somehow if you fight the system you're going to lose to it. That is basically the point. I don't care whether you're a painter or an architect you can't fight the system. In

my mind, if you fight the system it only means you want to join it. So it is very important that you do something you like, that you're involved in enough to hold your interest no matter how long it takes. If the film doesn't involve you, it's what we call "a stepping-stone" picture, you know, a stepping-stone to art, and that's all right too. Take a guy like Polanski who did pictures in Poland, *Knife in the Water*, and later *Repulsion*. You could see in those works a pulse that was meaningful and creative and intense. You can't dispute the fact that he's an artist, but yet you have to say that *Rosemary's Baby* is not art. It is a dictated design—boom, boom, boom, boom. People are used within that design to make a commercial product to sell to people. I'm not saying that is bad. I was in it. I'm fine. I'm happy. But it isn't art and I don't know, I think *Dirty Dozen* in its way is more artistic, you know, because it's compulsively going forward, trying to make something out of the moment without preordaining the way the outcome is going to be.

Loeb: How about you? How much design was there in *Woman Under the Influence*? Was the script in your hand when you started to shoot? It's very interesting for people to understand the process. How much improvisation was there?

Cassavetes: On *A Woman Under the Influence*, like on anything, you start off with an idea. It doesn't mean anything to you. It's just an idea. You can discuss it in your living room. And then if that idea stays with you for a while, at least if it does with me, then I feel I can spend a long time working on it, no matter what kind of inconvenience it would cause to my life. I got a lot of people together, because I knew we wouldn't have any money to make the picture. I got people off the streets and the first people that came up, they were our crew. I knew that if they would take the trouble to come up to see us, they would get involved and they would stay. I know a lot of actors, so I started out with some actors. We had a reading—Elaine May and I and Peter Falk read the plays that *Woman* was predicated on and Peter said he wanted to do it. And then he called me three days later and said that Mike Nichols just offered him a picture to do, *Day of the Dolphin*, starting November 15. "You don't have any money," he said, "and November is next month." I said, "You can't do it." He said, "Well, what do I tell Mike? He's the director. I can't just say I don't want to do the fish picture. You call him and tell him something. You're the writer, you can make something up." So, in the end we started with Peter. We started with Gena. We started with those people who had come in. And we had two very good friends of ours who were secretaries. They are very important. They write all the stuff down and do all the work and we take all the credit.

Every picture is different. It really depends strongly upon the people that you're working with. They must be your peers, people who could be your friends. Now I'm an older guy and I walk in the room and someone says, "Who is this?"

You know, "What's in it for me?" And that's fine. That's terrific. I've got to work with that guy and I've got to know that guy's capable of hating me and liking me and dealing with me as a person and telling me I'm full of shit if I am, and being able to take over the direction of the picture if he can, you know. If he can work harder than me or she can work harder than me, then they should do it. And what is a director, really? A director is a name. The people seek after it, they seek to be a director, or seek to be a cinematographer. If you go on a major studio picture, you'll see people who don't protect the picture. They protect themselves. I've seen guys and it has nothing to do with their talent—I've seen crews talk about loyalty. They say, "If they fire you, honey, then I'm going with you." I mean the whole crew is going to revolt if it doesn't go your way. But when the chips are down, they all say good-bye. I've never seen anyone go with anybody fired on a major picture. But when you're working for nothing, when you're working with friends, it doesn't happen that way. You have to have your own values. You have to want to make your own picture. You have to have your own image of making a picture, otherwise you're no help to anyone or to yourself. So I'm saying that an education in art has to come from working with other people who are connected in a sense with something they want to do and want to be.

Loeb: I have one specific question about the editing in *Woman*. There's a six-month interlude in the film. When did you decide to put it in? Was that a discovery in the editing room? John, it troubled me.
Cassavetes: Oh yeah. Elaine May didn't like that either. She begged me to take that out. I like it because I wanted to know how long Mabel was away.

Question: I wanted to see Peter Falk locked up, too.
Cassavetes: What do you mean you wanted to see him locked up?

Question: Well, he seemed really evil in the movie. It was easy to understand the title *A Woman Under the Influence* because everything that she did was an attempt to please him, but he was being destructive to her. In fact, he seemed nuttier than she.
Cassavetes: I don't think she was nutty.

Question: I don't think she was either. That's what I'm trying to say. I think he was.
Cassavetes: But we all are. Now I say that and I mean it, really. We're never nutty on film. That's the trouble with this world. On the screen everyone is perfect. They're a perfect heavy, they're a perfect good guy. That's boring.

Question: Recently I saw some outtakes of *Star Trek*. Spock or the perfect who-ever flubs and stutters or drops something that he's not supposed to. And it was nice to see this "perfect" person, this creation of a human being make a mistake. Could you comment on that since you mentioned that you don't like rigidity?

Cassavetes: The time limits are terrible on television productions. They want to give you the best product in the world, one that is technically right. If something doesn't match there's a script coordinator to correct it. It's usually a girl and she usually says, "He didn't say *the* man, he said the *man*." And so they go back again, do it perfectly, and then they cut it that way. It's unfortunate.

Question: In the morning-after scene, the guy Mabel picked up goes into the kitchen and has a cup of coffee, and then you see her husband pull up. What happened?

Loeb: It seemed like he just disappeared. You expect a confrontation. You expect *High Noon*. And also how did the mother find out that Mabel had a man over?

Cassavetes: A lot of people ask the same question. The Falk character told the mother. And how did he know? Listen, you have to assume that everybody has lived. Men and women both have an understanding of these things. If a man walks into his house and sees his wife sitting like that in a mood and he has lived with her for a number of years, he knows that something is wrong. I'm not inter-ested in pursuing that dramatically. I'm interested in the involvement between the mother and the son. And the mother does control that son, a grown man. He's forty-six years old and she comes into that house and she runs that house. And she asks Nick to commit this woman and he only commits her because she wants to. And she really feels that what Nick told her about Mabel is the truth. And then she adds her own truth to it and feels that the son can no longer live with this woman.

Question: Did you film a confrontation between Falk and the pick-up?

Cassavetes: No, never. Nor did I film a scene in which he told the mother about it. You know, when you're making a film, you deal with it somehow in a subjective view. I would rather not deal in terms of conventional expectations of what actu-ally happened. It didn't seem very emotionally important to me that Peter would tell his mother and we would see it.

Question: But what happened to the guy in the house? What actually happened to him?

Cassavetes: It wasn't a continuity cut. It's hard to tell jump cuts with me some-times. It was a time change. But it comes at a point, probably, where you really want to know how the guy got out of the house. For that reason, you might object to what I did. Anyway, you know what happens within a minute or two. Why should you know right away? You find out that the husband didn't see him.

Question: What was the main thing about the film that interested you, the main idea?

Cassavetes: The woman did—the problem of being alone after having been promised love—a good woman fulfilling her end of the promise and not getting any reward for it. I think the way our world is structured there is no room for women to have an education, an emotional education. I'm not saying that I would know how to give a woman an emotional education. But it is true that women do have problems being housewives, being married. And that is what interested me and everyone else who worked on the film. It was an exploration of the problems of women without really knowing what the answers are. We tried to pose as many questions as we could about love and its consequences.

Loeb: There is a scene of her waiting at the bus that is extraordinary. What a beautiful and devastating moment as she waits for her kids and you realize they're all that she has.

Question: There is another scene at the door, when everyone first comes over in the morning for spaghetti. I was wondering how did you get that out of Gena and the rest of the group? Was that ad-lib or was it scripted?

Cassavetes: That was a carefully rehearsed scene which came out of a lot of pre-rehearsing, pre-talking the picture. It's mainly Gena and those actors that were able to do that. It's hard to say why it works so well.

Question: There is a scene with the children when they are struggling with their father the night they decide to commit Mabel. I got the feeling that for some people that might have been very painful to watch because it was so involved and might reflect their own personal experience. Did you deliberately extend the sequence so that people would feel the pain more intensely?

Cassavetes: I think so. We did deliberately prolong it. I think the main reason that sequence was so full was because I felt very much like Tony said before. You can't go without a shootout. It's a very difficult thing for someone to double-cross somebody. Unless you actually see them do that, unless you actually see the continuity of that, the actual idea that he would do this and carry it through could have been weakened. And I didn't particularly like the scene upstairs. But I felt it was necessary for Nick to go upstairs and make up his mind that he would actually do this in the face of the children, in the face of his wife. It was very important that he actually decide to commit this woman so that it would become a memory for him. It's the hardest thing in the world to put someone that you love in an institution. There is a lot of pain involved.

Question: When you and Peter were discussing Nick's character, did you use *Husbands* as a take-off? Did that provide a point of reference?
Cassavetes: No.

Question: You saw them as two totally separate characters?
Cassavetes: Yes. You have to understand something. I would write it down and then I'd stay away from it so that the actor's intentions or additions could come clear. I allow the man, the actor, the actress, to be in touch with themselves and to draw on it. If the script is right, I don't think that they need any direction at all except their own.

Question: Were you aware of pacing at all when dealing with Peter? It seemed like almost every scene he was in would reach a fever pitch of intensity. Were you letting him reach his own peaks? How much were you controlling him in the film?
Cassavetes: I wasn't controlling him in the sense you mean. I certainly would have cautioned him if I felt he was wrong and if I felt he would be disliked. I feel that Peter is a magical kind of an actor in that he can take a person who is human and add to his humanity. Gena's character is really without pettiness throughout the whole picture, and until the very last scene in the movie, she really is under the influence of family and Nick. She's under the influence of her mother-in-law. She's under the influence of the love for her mother who doesn't like her but loves her, if you know what I mean. She's under the influence of a father who's disowned her because she's now married and so he's "given" her to the son-in-law. And I forgot what the question was.

Question: I feel that Nick's character was one-dimensional, and he responded in a visceral manner to every stimulus you presented him. He seemed to react that way in every scene.
Cassavetes: One of the things we had worked out in the beginning of the movie was that these characters could not be petty because you would lose the whole intention of what the film was about. Most of the arguments between men and women are based upon somebody's inability to express what they really mean. At least that is the way I feel. And that is the way the members of the cast felt, that when a man and a woman get together, they fight about the television—turn it on, turn it low, turn it up—drinking, etc. All the things that really count are very rarely expressed, no matter how long a marriage goes on, no matter how long the love goes on. Mabel's problem was that she had no self. Her problem was that she

was doing everything to please someone other than herself. When Nick wanted her to go to bed with him, she'd go to bed. When he wanted her to be embarrassed, she'd be embarrassed. If he wanted her to apologize, she'd apologize. He wanted her to be nice to guys coming in at eight o'clock in the morning—ten guys for spaghetti—well, OK. That is a man's dream for a woman to get up and say, "Yeah, let's cook it and have a good time." That is a man's dream, not a woman's dream, you know. But he couldn't control that friendship. He couldn't control the feelings of warmth and niceness that he instilled in her. I mean, here is a construction worker, a guy who goes out and works with his hands. He is a very formal guy. He believes in family and home. His mother really has a great influence over him. Relatives have a great influence over him. He is a conservative and all of a sudden he marries a girl. He takes the one little act of danger in his life. She is a little kooky. She is a little crazy. She loves him intensely. It is a little embarrassing to him. It is very embarrassing to him to display emotion. He doesn't want to display that emotion to the world. He doesn't want to have that closeness and that rapport with people. He wants distance in his public life and the only thing that can throw him off is this woman. And while he feels this thing in her to be unusual—crazy in bed, divinely kooky, whatever—he can't handle the results. He is living two different lives and he loves them both. And he has got it made. She is living one life. She waits for this man to come home. His life is falling apart through a series of embarrassments, the pull of family, the pull of his friends. How is he going to look in front of his friends when this woman carries on? At a certain point in the picture he falls out of love with her and that is why he has her committed.

Question: That was hard to take.

Cassavetes: Yeah. The point is that I don't believe any man can be told when he makes a jerk of himself, you know? Now that seems like a little thing. It is not shooting someone in the head or anything, but it can cause a hell of a lot of pain. That is the one moment of pettiness in the picture because he was really petty, dog, deep-down petty, you know, in the spaghetti scene. He was embarrassed. He couldn't come off it. He couldn't come down.

Now as an actor Peter became very passive when we did the scene with the doctor. Those were peculiar choices that he made. When the doctor came in he had the freedom to throw him out. But he chose to let him in. Peter also had the freedom not to stand by and let his wife go crazy, but he chose to let her go crazy. And when he came upon her and tried to stop her, it was too late and he knew it was too late and why did he wait that long? Now in talking with Peter afterwards, Peter said, "She was doing great. I didn't want to stop her." That was a lie. Peter is a tremendously internal man, and I think he wanted her to be committed. I think he wanted her to go away. I don't think he recognized her worth because to him at that moment she was worthless. She wasn't behaving like he would behave so he didn't want her anymore. That is what I saw. Now within the values of his getting upset, within the values of his being too loud, too boisterous, whatever these actions were by a man who was not used to functioning outside himself, outside the boundaries, without his control. When he went out to the work area the day after she was committed, I really felt he was shocked that anyone would give a shit that Mabel went to an institution. Who was she that anyone would care? Why would anyone like her? Who was she? She was a product of his imagination. She wasn't a person. She was a person who did exactly what he said. She was a kook. She was known as a nut. So he didn't like to be discovered. He didn't like it when the guys said something because he felt enormously guilty for it.

Now it is very complicated to structure that. The emotions are complicated. It is hard to explain because they are hard messages to get over to anybody. So you have to allow the actor total freedom, not a little freedom. Don't say, "Improvise your emotions," and then stop and say, "Wait a minute, buddy, if you could do this it would be good, and by the way, go back to what you were doing before." It won't work. So what you do is you let that actor run with it. He grows with the part. He is making a fool of himself and he is making a jerk of himself and he is becoming more transparent. So by the time you get him to the beach—the beach scene, I think, is wonderful and Peter is wonderful because he absolutely has no idea what he is doing there. I had the camera down there and they just started walking. I never went near them and they are walking and Peter has some lines and he says the lines and then they don't know what to do. Now I could tell them but that would kill it. What difference does it make what he does? He has to do it. I can't do it. The camera can move. It can follow, you know. So where they play that scene and what they do has to be in their own timing. And when Peter gets there at the beach and he pushes the little girl down, there was a wonderful moment. I see him trying to communicate with his children. I see him trying to touch. I see him not caring. I see so many things that developed that wouldn't have if you formalized a view of the character through your own mind and didn't allow room for interpretation. I wrote it and as soon as I wrote it, I killed the writer. There is no writer because the writer can only make you feel insecure. I have been in a lot of movies and as soon as the writer would come on the set everyone died. Because the writer knows exactly how everyone should be played, exactly what the intentions are. But writing is one medium and film is another medium.

Question: How do you separate yourself?
Cassavetes: You do one thing at a time. After we finish with the film we distribute it. But we don't distribute the film while we're making the film, you know.

Loeb: Well, what about your overall intention, the overall strategy. It has to stay controlled. You have a tragedy. It's a high-powered thing.

Cassavetes: Why is it a tragedy?

Loeb: Well, I felt that Falk never reached a moment of understanding, a perception of what was wrong in that house. When I walked out of the theater I had the distinct impression that it's going to happen again. That saddened the hell out of me. She tried to cut her wrists tonight and next week she'll do it again because no one understood. Without insight, the triangle will continue.

Cassavetes: All right. That's the point of the whole picture. Now we're down to the difference, maybe, between the way it should be and the way it is, you know? That is the point of the picture. That is what we tried to do. There is the outside world and there is the inside world. The inside world is your home, your family, the things that create emotions within you. The outside world is you and where you are going and how you move and where you fly, you know? And they are two worlds. I really believe, after making the picture, not before, that the inside world really holds you, really contains you, can cause you pain that you don't show outside and that is why no one ever talks about it.

I think Nick changed. I think he has perception. I think he has insight. The simple act of throwing his mother and father and everybody out at that end—it may not be a big thing for a less structured person, but it was a very big thing for him to clear everybody out and mean it. I think he came to the realization that he was alone with that woman. He was the only one who could save that woman or kill that woman or have anything to do with that woman, and that it was a one-to-one relationship. People prefer distance and in movies today there is a reluctance to show really deep feelings. They don't like vulnerability. No one is willing to be laughed at. Nobody wants to be laughed at. Let's laugh. I spilled stuff on my tie tonight. Why should you guys not laugh at me because I look like a dope. Why should I take offense at that? The only reason I would was if I don't like you and you don't like me. Now that's a crazy assumption to make—that no one likes anybody, and we sometimes live under that assumption.

Question: When you script your films, how specific are you? How do you anticipate the improvisation?

Cassavetes: The idea is that they, the characters, can do whatever they want to within the confines of the script.

Question: Well, what is the script, then?

Cassavetes: A script is a series of words strung together. They kind of spell out the story in a mysterious way.

Question: What is the process like for you when you're doing the script? Is it like acting for you? Do you say, "I know these people so well I can tell you everything they're going to do?"

Cassavetes: No, I deal with the characters as any writer would deal with a character. There are certain characters that you like, that you have feeling for, and other characters stand still. So you work until you have all the people in some kind of a motion, you know?

Question: How do you deal with the time lag between the idea and the time it takes to pull it off? Is the wait frustrating for you?

Cassavetes: You do get tired, frustrated. You hate the project but you want to go on. Something drives you and that's usually the other people involved. Their determination adds to yours. When they drift off, you come on again. It goes back and forth.

Question: Did you have trouble raising the funds for this?

Cassavetes: I got Gena and Peter to put up all the money.

Loeb: How have your films done financially? How did *Husbands* do at the box office?

Cassavetes: *Husbands* grossed $1.4 million. Columbia paid us $3.5 million for it. I don't think they ever liked the film. After they first bought it, we all took it to the San Francisco Film Festival. The day we got the check we went up there and everything was supposed to be terrific. But after the film came on everyone yelled "Fascist." They were booing and they were going crazy. Here is this whole row of Columbia executives and their wives, and the wives turn to the executives and say, "What is wrong, why are they booing?" The audience got worse. They got hostile, eighteen hundred people really booing. The terrible part is that you have to get up after the film ends. There are chairs there, the microphone is there, and the people yell, "Fascist." I had a suit on. I felt like ripping it off. You don't know what to say so you say, "How did you like the film?" Absolute silence. Finally, one guy said, "If you guys were making a satire about the middle class and how piggish they are, that is one thing. But if those guys depicted on the screen are really like you, that's another." And I said, "It is us . . . it's us" and Peter said, "That's right . . . that's right." Well, we thought we were going to be killed. It was getting terrific. The only friends we had were Gena and Seymour who were in the audience, in the back. Anytime anybody said something, Gena would shout, "Sit down." A guy would get up and yell and Seymour would say "bullshit." Anyway, you don't always win with a film. But I still like it and I will always remember the experience of that film and how much enjoyment I had in working with Peter Falk and Ben Gazzara.

Question: I don't understand why you say this film is a failure?
Cassavetes: To the studio, at least. A financial failure.

Loeb: I thought it was an extraordinary picture. The fantasy of men, their essential childishness, is captured so well.
Cassavetes: Well, we did wonderfully well in New York. For some reason, New Yorkers liked the picture.

Question: Maybe it was a success after all—to move that many people, even to anger, is something. People often don't want to see truth. It is too painful. It's hard to tolerate.
Cassavetes: I'm not sure about that. I think when the picture came out it was boring to many people.

Question: What is your favorite film?
Cassavetes: *Shadows*.

Loeb: That was your first film. Can you talk about it a moment before we close?
Cassavetes: *Shadows* was finished in 1960. It took three years or so. We were so dumb when we made that picture. I was the director so I said "print" and everyone said "print" and no one kept a record. We did everything wrong, technically. The only thing we did right was to get a group of people together who were young, full of life and wanting to do something of meaning. I saw it recently, for the first time in a long time. I saw all those people on the screen, you know. Young and beautiful and just full of life and everything and it made me emotional, especially seeing Rupert Crosse up there because suddenly he was so alive and it was terrific. He died recently of cancer. He was supposed to be in *The Last Detail* and he died. I got up recently to talk about the film at the American Film Institute. We saw it together and I cried at the end. I saw Rupert and it just hit me. I stood up before everyone and had trouble talking. I don't know. Anyway, thank you everybody for coming here.

A Director of Influence, John Cassavetes

Gautam Dasgupta / 1975

From *Film* (London) 26 (May 1975): 4–6. Reprinted by permission of Gautam Dasgupta.

John Cassavetes was born in New York City in 1929. He trained for the stage at the American Academy of Dramatic Arts and gained prominence early in life as a television and screen actor. In the fifties he began working for television and appeared as the lead in *Omnibus* and played other significant roles in over one hundred shows. He also starred in his own television series *Johnny Staccato*. With *The Night Holds Terror* (1953), Cassavetes embarked on his film acting career. Since then he has worked under such directors as Sidney Lumet, John Frankenheimer, Roman Polanski, Robert Aldrich, Don Siegel, and Elaine May. Recently he appeared in *Rosemary's Baby* and *The Dirty Dozen* for which he received an Academy Award nomination as Best Supporting Actor.

In 1958, Cassavetes started an acting workshop in New York. *Shadows*, his first attempt at film directing, grew out of the workshop exercises developed by the actors and students over a period of two years. The film opened to critical acclaim in London in 1961 and won several awards at major European Film Festivals. This was followed by a few abortive directorial ventures for Paramount and it wasn't until 1969 that Cassavetes emerged on his own with *Faces*, a success both in America and abroad. Soon after he completed *Husbands* (1970) and *Minnie and Moskowitz* (1971). *A Woman Under the Influence* (1974) is his most recent film and stars Gena Rowlands and Peter Falk.

A Woman Under the Influence tells the story of a disturbed housewife as she desperately seeks affection and acceptance by those around her. Played with consummate artistry and perfection by Gena Rowlands in the role of Mabel Longhetti ("It was the greatest part I ever had in my acting career"), the film tirelessly searches for the emotional truths that bind Mabel to her children and to her blue-collar husband Nick, played with equal skill by Peter Falk. Cassavetes regards it as his "most optimistic" film to date.

Gautam Dasgupta: What was the initial motive behind the making of *A Woman Under the Influence*?

John Cassavetes: Quite simply, an absolute desire to make this film. Those of us working in the film industry are all reporters in one sense or another. We report from a certain editorial point of view on what we feel, on what we see, and on what is important to us. The most important thing in my life, in Gena's life, and in the lives of our intimate friends was the idea of marriage. We were deeply concerned with the change in illusions that marriage engenders over a period of years and the overwhelming need to understand the problems of retaining the family. Out of that came the characters, the feelings for the characters, and, in a more specific sense, the complex delineation of the woman in the film. The problems confronting women today are the insanity that they feel, the deep frustrations created by the changes in social behavior that are new to them.

Dasgupta: What role do the children play in the conception of this film?

Cassavetes: Children grow up with innocence and an instinctive love for the people they care about. Firm in their emotional commitments and thrust into the middle of changes in their immediate surroundings, they are in a particularly traumatic situation. Their permanence and fixity of purpose contrasted with the ongoing flux of a domestic household seemed to be a very good subject for a film.

Dasgupta: Does *A Woman Under the Influence* represent a break with the thematic concerns of your earlier films?

Cassavetes: I don't know whether it has anything to do with my age or experience, but at this point in life I choose to think in terms of consideration. Earlier films, such as *Shadows* and *Husbands*, grew out of personal experiences reaching all the way back to my childhood days. They were expressions of my innermost feelings, and now that I've dealt with all that, I feel obligated to view life in other terms. I've come to recognize the errors of my own ways perhaps, the selfishness and the insensitivities of my past, but mind you I'm in no way putting these down. From an actor's and a director's point of view these are wonderful things—his art is forged from them. It's just that now I recognize things I had eliminated from my life and *A Woman Under the Influence* is an appreciation of those other values in familial and social relationships.

Dasgupta: Critics and audiences have hailed it a "Woman's Picture."

Cassavetes: I make films about people, about social relationships. I strongly believe that we are social animals and the nature of living is defined not by money, political power, and the like, but by virtue of the fact that we are social beings. Within such a system men have always been in a more favorable position—they are allowed to test themselves against the rest of the world since they are in contact with it. Women, like Mabel in the film, can go mad simply because they are isolated in their homes. Mabel must find out what others are thinking just so that she may gain a feeling for life. She doesn't even necessarily have to like the others or be comfortable with them. It is only by interacting with them, by engaging in some sort of a competition with others that she feels alive. The emphasis here is both on the woman and on society—the pressures and influences exerted by society on Mabel. And furthermore, this picture was shot primarily from a woman's point of view.

Dasgupta: Did that necessitate a change in your approach to the film?
Cassavetes: Not particularly, except in so far as the film was shot in color. For a woman, the world outside is in some ways a fantasy world, a realm removed from the confines of her home. Furthermore, about 80 percent of the movie was shot indoors and the rest of it amidst vast exteriors—beaches, mountainsides, etc. I somehow felt that the characters were strong enough to need the enlargement of the scope of reality.

Dasgupta: Since *Husbands*, all your films have been in color.
Cassavetes: *Husbands* was once again a fantasy, a present-day, real-life fantasy. *Minnie and Moskowitz* was a pure fantasy and to shoot it in black and white would have been pretentious. If I ever film a gangster story I'd probably do it in black and white or else no one would believe it. Personally, I feel that any picture in black and white is going to look better than in color. I did make a slop print of *A Woman Under the Influence* in black and white, but after seeing it in color I realized that there were certain values greater in the color print.

Dasgupta: The spontaneity in *A Woman Under the Influence* suggests that the film may have been improvised.
Cassavetes: No, the entire script was written and there were no improvisations whatsoever.

Dasgupta: How are the actors directed in this film?
Cassavetes: I very rarely tell an actor what to do. Being an actor I know well enough that it's presumptuous to tell a person how he or she should behave in a particular situation. I do like to place the actor in a controlled situation where the only way the person can react is in an emotional manner. I suppose at times I trick actors, but it goes beyond that. I am prepared to kill any actor that won't reveal himself. So the characters only partake in what I consider emotional improvisation within the confines of a given situation. They don't create the situation

but strive to realize the emotional complexities that create a rich and compelling character.

Dasgupta: Isn't this technique far removed from the improvisatory structure of your first film *Shadows*?
Cassavetes: Yes, but again there were two versions of that film. When I had completed the first version, we (Jonas Mekas and I) looked at the result of a beautiful experiment which I'd worked on for over two years. Although I was not unproud of it, the film did seem to be excessively indulgent. I had intellectually satisfied myself completely in terms of an expression, but all expression should be communicative and can be relayed to the audience only by making it emotionally concentrated. The emotional expressiveness of the first version, I felt, was dissipated in its generality—the emotions were not precise and particularized. The second version was more exact.

Dasgupta: Parker Tyler once stated that your "camera style is built around the actor as character constructor." It is evident that you make great use of close-ups, hand-held shots and "cinéma-vérité" techniques. Can you comment on this?
Cassavetes: To be frank, these are all expressions for critics and cinema buffs. To look at a film intellectually or be proud of it in light of its stylistic ingredients is an attitude that I rarely care to indulge in. As an artist I am not concerned with whether I'm a "cinéma-vérité director or not. If "cinéma-vérité" translates as truthful cinema, then yes, I'm trying to put down on celluloid a certain truth. I aim to provide my audiences with a sense of immediacy, the here and the now, and an enlargement to which they can relate.

Dasgupta: Do you use the camera as a "psychiatric tool"?
Cassavetes: The camera seeks to capture the subtle and minute changes in human behavior that make us what we are. I refuse to let myself or my characters seek refuge in psychology either for purposes of motivation or character analysis.

Dasgupta: Do you feel that your films are tragic or comic?
Cassavetes: I don't think there is such a thing as tragedy. There is living and dying and in between the search for an answer as to how we are to fill the brief moments of life. The films are a road map through emotional and intellectual terrains that provide a solution to how one can save pain. Nor are they comic in the sense of being romantic. As people we know that we are petty, vicious, violent, and horrible, but my films make an effort to contain the depression within us and to limit the depression to those areas that we can actually solve. The comic resolution of my films, if one could at all call it that, is the assertion of a human spirit.

Dasgupta: Do you attempt to create a moral universe in your films?

Cassavetes: I am a moralist in that I believe the greatest morality is to acknowledge the freedom of others; to be oneself and not to be in judgment of others who are different from you. Filmmaking to me is an investigation of what is in someone's mind. I absolutely refuse to judge the characters in my films and it is imperative that the characters neither analyze themselves nor others during the course of the filming. I refrain from leading people by their noses by not imposing a stereotyped moral vision on my work.

Dasgupta: Your philosophy wavers between the sentimental and idealistic visions of a Frank Capra on the one hand and the harsh and honest realizations of the Italian neorealists on the other.

Cassavetes: I adore Frank Capra. He was and still is, in my opinion, the greatest filmmaker that ever lived. Capra created a feeling of belief in a free country and that there is goodness in bad people; that everyone reaches a limit where they would stop and be sane again because what they really wanted was to have compassion for other people and live in a spirit of friendliness and brotherhood. I don't think his films were sentimental or romantic; they were expressions of a practical philosophy. Like him I believe that there cannot be artists who find no room for elemental human behavior and passion. Idealism is not sentimental; it validates a hope for the future. Capra gave me hope and in turn I wish to extend a sense of hope to my audiences. By affording the spectators a glimpse into ideas that confuse, rock, and disturb them, I offer the mind food for thought. An aesthetic experience that leaves the spectator vacant is no form of art.

At the same time I don't emulate Capra. The characters in my films display a lack of comfort and find themselves in petty and embarrassing situations, but this is only so because they haven't yet come to grips with their emotional natures. I am a tough and deeply cynical person. Capra didn't care about his cynicism. I wish I could be as independent as him to really express the beautiful ideas he could without feeling perhaps that these ideas were not truthful. If I had the capacity, the means, and the temperament, I would love to make every one of Capra's films but so far I've never done it.

Dasgupta: And the neorealists?

Cassavetes: I certainly adore the neorealists for their humaneness of vision. Zavattini is surely the greatest screenwriter that ever lived. Particularly inspirational to me were *I Vitelloni*, *Umberto D*, and *Bellissima*. The neorealist filmmakers were not afraid of reality; they looked it straight in the face. I have always admired their courage and their willingness to show us how we really are. It's the same with Godard, early Bergman, Kurosawa, and the second greatest director next to Capra, Carl Dreyer.

Dasgupta: Do you find that your films are distinctly American somewhat in the manner of Capra's *Mr. Deeds Goes to Town*, *Meet John Doe*, etc.?

Cassavetes: The films are certainly expressive of a culture that has had the possibility of attaining material fulfillment while at the same time finding itself unable to accomplish the simple business of conducting human lives. We have been sold a bill of goods as a substitute for life. What is needed is a reassurance in individual emotions; a reevaluation of our emotional capacities. I feel that people are ultimately individuals and it's only when they are trained to fit into a sociological pattern that is convenient to someone that they begin to blame their conditions even up to being born. Like Capra, I make films about the individual who asserts himself or herself in the face of a multitude.

I want my films to reflect a truly democratic spirit and I find myself siding with the lone minority. I love the ethnic groups in our country—the Italians, for instance, like the Longhettis of the film—and am pained to find that they are willing to settle for a mediocrity and trade in their uniqueness for white-collar materialistic existence. To change the world we must start with human behavior, the human spirit, and isn't that what Capra's films were all about.

Dasgupta: Where do you go from here?

Cassavetes: At the present moment, if I want to make a film I have to be desperate about it. I feel that my filmic life has come to some kind of an end. I doubt if I'll be making films very long because I've done it the best way I know how. As an artist I feel that we must try different things—but above all we must dare to fail. I want to explore other areas of human and artistic experiences. I don't know what the future has in store for me and that's the fun of it. I simply love life—from one golden moment to the next.

Interview with John Cassavetes

Michel Ciment and Michael Henry / 1976

From *Positif,* April 1976. Reprinted by permission.

Q: You said once that *Faces* was much longer than the version audiences are familiar with. Is *A Woman Under the Influence* similarly reduced?

A: All my films are long. With age, we become more complicated, we see more aspects of reality. When you make your first film, everything is pure, you're enthusiastic, filled with both constructive and destructive impulses, and you don't give a damn about anybody. With the second film you realize how difficult this task is. By the third you have to find a method of working where what you want to say makes sense in emotional terms. I don't edit my films to please anybody, but so that the audience understands the human aspects of the film better, and so that the film relates to them and not just to myself. Because all my films are of course personal. Dissolving marriages, love that degenerates into betrayal, the difficulty two people have continuing to communicate well once they live together—these are problems I've had to come to grips with personally, but that also concern others. Sometimes people find that too painful to accept, or think my point of view is skewed, or just simply aren't interested in how difficult it is to communicate with others. But it interests me. With my actors, I try to explore all that and to convert it into terms that align with people's daily life and experiences.

Q: *A Woman Under the Influence* also must have been something of an ordeal. How do you direct a million-dollar film outside the system?

A: There's a different economic solution for each film. With *Faces* and *Shadows*, we all pitched in. For *A Woman Under the Influence*, the crew worked for a little pay, and it was decided without a contract that if we made money, we'd give it to them. That's what happened. I work with my friends, with people I like, and we're comfortable with each other because we have the same goals. What we're looking for is to express feelings and emotions. Many potential colleagues would be thinking about their careers or of their next projects and wouldn't dream of stopping everything for two or three years. This doesn't bother me. Of course, I think about it too, but only after the film is over. For *A Woman Under the Influence*, Peter Falk, Gena, and I invested our own money into the film.

Q: In your work, your sequences are quite long. How much of what you shoot do you keep after editing? Do you dispense with entire sequences or do you prefer to make reductions within each sequence?

A: I've cut entire sequences. For example, in *A Woman Under the Influence*, there were many scenes in which Gena and Peter were alone together. I loved what passed between them in these scenes. There was also a really pretty scene in the morning, where they shared their dreams of the previous night and another one where they walked in the rain. Watching the film from beginning to end, I realized that unconsciously perhaps I was giving the public what they wanted, something that surely corresponded to a romantic wish on my part, and on the part of my actors, that their relationship follow a fictional style. But my film is not romantic. Because marriage is not completely a "romance" according to me! Those moments where we have time to be romantic are very sparse in a marriage. Basically, the relationship of these two people was so intimate in these scenes that one wouldn't otherwise be able to believe in their fundamental crisis. So I gave up those scenes. The first cut was three hours and fifty minutes.

Q: *A Woman Under the Influence* is your most simple film in terms of the storyline. There are hardly any new factual events introduced over the course of the film. Everything is set at the beginning and everything unfolds at an emotional level.

A: Almost everyone has either been married or in love. In this type of subject, we start with the viewer's experience. These days, doctors also work from reasonable assumptions. In a film, it's pointless to repeat everything people know from experience. When a man leaves for work at nine in the morning and doesn't return until seven at night, his wife is alone, she's going to go shopping, take care of the kids, watch television, read a book, play cards with friends. The only thing left to show is the conditions existing between this man and woman, who don't judge each other like most couples do, who live together with an enormous acceptance of each other and who nonetheless suffer greatly in their marriage and in their infidelity. And there is the pain felt by this woman who lives under the influence of a man, which isn't fair, but it exists. Love has an influence: if you love someone you want them to be faithful, that they take care of you, that they love you, you insist on so much from the other that you ask the impossible. And suddenly everything falls apart because each person forgets the other, takes them for granted, thinks with total certainty that they will always be the same when they come back, they don't worry about the other's problems right up until the moment when they become aware of them, and brutally so.

Q: I get the feeling that for you, to make a film is to create reality rather than to reproduce it. What part does improvisation play in your work?

A: I'm so skilled that you don't realize it, but everything is scripted! (laughter) It would be very different if it was improvised. We deal with thoughts and feelings, and my hope is that the actors don't feel it as it's written. So that they won't think about the words, they'll take their time and the words will become a part of them. Sometimes, of course, an actor comes to me and says, "My character wouldn't do this." And I tell them to not do it. There is no obligation on their end. Very often lines of dialogue are cut. I never see an actor forget their dialogue or feel obligated to say a line. I let them do what they want, always. In *Shadows* and *Husbands* there was lots of improvisation, but everything was written in advance for *Faces*, *Minnie and Moskowitz*, and *A Woman Under the Influence*. But for me the outcome is the same.

Q: Do you change the script during rehearsal?

A: Very often, if it's not working. If you have a good actor yet get to a point where he can't act, it's because your script is weak, the writing doesn't work, or the intentions of the scene aren't clear. I don't think I'm perfect, by any means. Each morning I wake up and tell myself I'm not so sure of my own life that I can speak about others' marriages. During rehearsals we talk to one another and sometimes rewrite entire sequences. In most films the actors don't even meet each other. Once I acted in a film and found out afterwards that this or that actor acted in it as well. In my films, we come together over several weeks, sometimes at night for example, and we read the script together. We like each other a lot, we know each other and we work together over a long period. The actors come with suggestions and I ask them to write them down sometimes since sometimes I don't understand what they want to say. Gena, for example, read the final script and told me, "I hate this woman. What is she doing, what clothes is she wearing?" I told her at this point I didn't give a damn what she wears. But for her, it's important and she's right, it's me who made a superficial comment. So before starting the film, I visited about fifty homes of working couples. I knew what I was going to see and I knew that I wouldn't be happy with it: furniture covered in plastic, a nice kitchen, a nice car, outwardly neat but not much else, not lived in. Almost no art, no interest in music. And for entertainment, a family visit to McDonald's at the end of the week for a hamburger. I'm an artist and I don't live this way. Therefore I have to convert this into acceptable terms that also stay true to those for whom I'm speaking. The set designer found a big house, even though workers' houses aren't normally large. So we decided that the house was given to Nick by his parents. We could change reality without justifying the changes each time, because the house was a gift. Then, we decorated it according to the characters: sports trophies, kids' pictures. Everyone had their ideas. For example, should the house be painted? So the front was painted, but since the outside of the back was under construction, Nick could have gotten it painted by friends in exchange for a couple beers, but since he was too concerned with his family life, he left it as it was. Along with these elements we brought to the actors, they became more and more interested in the clothes they were going to wear, on the influence money had on them, on the life of their kids, why they slept on the ground floor, etc. Everything was discussed, nothing came solely from me.

Q: Why did you choose an Italian background?
A: In America, construction workers are Black or Mexican on the West Coast, and Italians, Portuguese, or Irish on the East Coast. But I think that the man could have been from some completely different ethnic background.

Q: But it's important in the film.
A: Yes, for the conflicts. She's of Swedish origin. But I don't know much more about Sweden than second or third generation Swedish people do. They know two or three words and eat a smorgasbord once a week while telling some old stories. It's a fantasy to conceive of the American "melting pot" as a sum of European cultures. Italian Americans go to Italy and are happy there but in fact they are happier in America, because that's where they have their Little Italy, where Venetians, Napolitanos, Sicilians feel unified, while in Italy they didn't get along with each other.

Q: As a child, were you aware of being a part of the Greek community?
A: No, not really. I was as proud of my cultural origins as I would have been with any other ethnicity. My parents spoke Greek, still speak Greek, and I also speak Greek, but poorly! I was born in New York, but my parents went back to Greece and I didn't return to America until I was eight. They told me at school that I didn't know English, that I only knew Greek. For me, language is simply written symbols. The language barrier has no meaning for me. People's emotions are the same everywhere.

Q: In your films, you often deal with the middle class, or even the working class, which is rare in American film. What reasons do you have for exploring these class environments?
A: These classes don't interest me more than others do. Perhaps these issues are related to world politics, but not my personal life. It doesn't matter to me if someone works with his hands or in international finance. Above all, for me it's about people I meet. I'm stubborn above all, but it's a very widespread idea in my

country in particular that the public isn't interested in characters that aren't rich. And the working classes themselves, it seems, would have no interest in seeing itself on screen. This is perhaps true. But that doesn't concern me with this film. In my experience, a wife has taken care of the children herself, and if she was very wealthy this wouldn't be a problem. In the working class, a wife is closer to her household. That's why I chose this environment, because it creates an emotional relationship with her children. When one is in a closed context, one is closer to one's family, one has greater problems with them. If you were wealthier, you would have other problems.

Q: This is the first of your films where one of your characters appears to have a mental disorder. Were there particular problems involved in illustrating this?
A: Listen, I'm half crazy myself. And I think that everyone is close to insanity but doesn't want to admit it, and we pretend that it's the others who are wrong and that we're in possession of the truth. I firmly believe that any wife, even though she loves her husband, if she's been married for a length of time doesn't know where to put her emotions, and that can drive her crazy. Some of them find an outlet, decide to be independent, for example. This particular woman believes intensely that when one is a good spouse, some reciprocity should transpire, but she doesn't quite know what it is. She's not really crazy, just frustrated beyond a level we can imagine. She doesn't know what to do, and above all, she's inept emotionally and in social relationships. Everything she does is an expression of her individuality but she doesn't know how to behave around others. In this sense, she's like all of us.

Q: Don't you think that stems from the fact that she has to play a number of roles: the good wife, the good mother, etc., and that ultimately she snaps?
A: I don't think she ever changes, that she cracks up. She's always been lucid. She's very direct, like women are—in fact, more direct than men, which is offensive to them. The husband looks ridiculous when he returns home annoyed that his children are naked. It's he that is behaving strangely. Based on past experience, he's come to the conclusion that something's going on when in fact, nothing is going on. She's trying to entertain a neighbor, taking her kids into the backyard so they can dance "Swan Lake" and faced with the embarrassment of her guest, she starts to behave crazily in order to distract her. But there's really nothing wrong with her behavior.

Their relationships are really those of men and women that we see every day. One day I tell myself this is the best life I've ever had, and the next minute, I want to kill myself or I want someone to kill me! For me, life is difficult and full of the mystery of the unknown, and what I'm going to feel any given moment. Half of life is comprised of unanticipated moods.

Q: In the first scene where they find themselves together, they communicate via a fascinating series of private gestures. This seems to be a crisis, an exceptional scene, but at the same time, we get the feeling that they often "talk" this way. This must have been due to a large extent on improvisation by the actors, right?

A: Yes. In a film, everyone finds inspiration in the moment. Of course, the scene was written. The words were there, but two great actors can express more with their loving relationship than by simply speaking lines. In order to interpret, they make choices: love and expect something to happen, or don't wait for anything, find significance or not, make demands or not. This is how they come to believe in their characters and express them. This man is embarrassed at his wife's peculiar behavior, and at the same time he likes it. But he doesn't want her to reveal herself this way to others; however, at the same time he invites them in at seven in the morning when she's going to behave this way . . . their relationships are therefore a series of contradictions.

Q: The fact that you have such significant variety in actors' emotions must cause problems for you as a director on set, in order to show such moments between them. Is it that the climate is already established by the relationships you've created among and with the actors, or rather do you give them direction before the cameras roll?

A: For me, anyone can be an actor. We're aware that we can play make-believe since our childhoods. I never tell an actor that they're acting it wrong. That it doesn't match up with my idea of what their performance should be. I trust an actor more when they give me their interpretation. Of course, if he's lazy or doesn't take his role seriously, in that case, I take a knife, my handgun, or my fist, and I kill them. I think I have one talent, as a director, to create an atmosphere where people can act naturally in the given situation. I don't try to control the set, which is often noisy, anarchic, the actors ganging up on me. On the other hand, I like directing a film with a sense of continuity. Ideally, the last scene should be as difficult to direct as the first as far as the work is concerned! This is the reason why I don't work with a large film company who, for budgetary reasons, cuts up the script into sections without taking chronology into account.

Q: How many cameras do you use?
A: Basically one. Sometimes two for external shots.

Q: Do you ever think, if need be, of returning to 16mm?

A: I don't work in 16mm anymore. My opinion of it has dropped. More and more there's no difference except it's easier to edit in 35mm. Camera movement is the same, so that doesn't change the shooting.

Q: But in 35mm you rediscovered the granular aspect you get with 16mm film.
A: I think that's true. I've never liked metallic colors, "hard" film, even back when it was fashionable—it leaves nothing to the imagination, nothing hidden. When *Shadows* was made we used long focal lengths because we didn't have a dolly to follow the actors. Sound, in Hollywood films, has a crystalline clarity. In *Shadows*, we filmed in the street, the sound was bad, you could hear all sorts of noise and people were shocked. But me, I don't know how to get a "pure" sound. I remember all the time we spent in the editing room trying to get rid of all those marvelous sounds. And now that's the fashion!

Q: Do you do lots of takes?
A: It varies. Sometimes very few. There are scenes where the actors don't trust you because they've been double-crossed many times by directors who changed their character in order to fit the story. I think it's difficult to get people to trust you to let them be what they want, to let them reveal themselves.

Q: How did you adjust your camera movements to the movement of the actors? How much was planned in advance? The film seems more controlled than your earlier films.
A: I think that the story is pretty simple. I wouldn't want to make a lot of cuts because I don't think you would believe the emotions that would be stimulated by technical ideas. We lit up the entire room and set up the camera to be open to the actors who would use the entire space. If you see something as convincing, then it doesn't matter how it's done. It's the quality of what you see that matters. If it's good, then the scene is good, even if the frame is bad. Each director would film the same scene in a different way. What I try to do is to anticipate the movement of the scene, to leave the actors as free as possible in the space. I can't demand that the actors fit their motion to a preplanned camera movement. They could only make it work by repetition, but that's boring and tiring, and the crew starts to become their audience. Then if the crew is bored, the actors feel like they're not doing well. Because of this, I try to make everything happen quickly. I shoot with long focal length lenses and make sure the sets have space and depth. I hate the idea that a film is created by the framing or the camera. I've watched scenes captured with seven or eight different angles; they were always good if the scene was good, they're always lousy if the scene was lousy. For me, what's important is to convince the public and yourself that what's happening on screen is really

happening. In some cases I would have preferred that some films have worse framing or be less good technically, so that they would be better! I don't try to adapt scenes to the camera but the camera to the scenes. The problem boils down to this: what's the best way to see the scene? Certain scenes were overexposed but that didn't matter much to me since the scene was good, and also that added a sense of sterility to the atmosphere, of fatigue and sadness.

Q: When writing Gena Rowlands's role, you gave her a much different character to play than earlier roles. With each film, you show a different side of her.
A: I think she's a great actress. It's difficult to say so because she's my wife, but I think she's capable to play whatever she wants. She's a very simple woman, straightforward, not nervous, very serious and she feels things very deeply. Working with her is marvelous.

Q: Is there a situation which gives you an incentive to make a particular film, or want to create a certain character?
A: It's the theme which intrigues me. So Gena and I are going to do another film about an actress, but I want the public to understand what an actress's life is like. We're going to discuss it together before I write the script. I take all our conversations into account: we talked about who's going to play the psychiatrist, but since she couldn't relate to that, I didn't bother; on the other hand, the interpreter is a female character so that directly concerned her, and I didn't choose without speaking to her first. If I hadn't, that would have affected the inspiration for her performance.

Q: Did you use the same mix of amateurs and professionals in your most recent film? What attracts you about this chemistry?
A: Gena and Peter are both extremely professional and I think the amateurs help them stay fresh. A professional actor has a tendency to disregard life sometimes, to think that their own problems are all important. An amateur in a small part can come in and attract attention, and when they succeed, it can cause the professional to wake up. For example, Lynn Carlin, who played the woman in *Faces*, had never acted before. In this film the ratio of amateurs to professionals was 50/50. But in fact today, how do you tell someone that they're an amateur, without defining it as someone who doesn't get paid?

Q: Only in *Husbands* did you yourself play an important role. Did that raise any particular problems for you?
A: When making that film, I wasn't at all bothered by it. But watching it I realized

that it was difficult. It wasn't a problem when I wasn't in the same scene as Peter Falk and Ben Gazzara.

Q: Have you thought about forming a repertory troupe?
A: Yes, when I was young. It was a dream of mine. But now I don't think about it anymore. I have to confront one film after another and do my best.

Q: In some way your films seem to be made as a reaction against your acting career. What do you carry over from that experience, positively or negatively?
A: I've never been considered as a director, except in the past few years. And I never thought of myself that way. Now that I've directed a significant number of films it would be bogus to act as if I wasn't a filmmaker. It's ridiculous to deny what puts bread on my table, my profession. But at the beginning I just wanted to enjoy what I was making and share it with others. It didn't matter if the film was ultimately a success, what mattered was the enjoyment of making it together. Then we started asking ourselves whether we were showing emotions clearly enough for audiences to react to them, or if it was too difficult. Most of my colleagues in California didn't have this point of view. They wanted to make the best possible film. That really wasn't my ambition, what I wanted was that the film make me happy, that it challenge some feelings that I have or that others have, that the actors have decent parts, that people express themselves with a certain dignity, or if they're making fools of themselves.

Q: When you worked in Hollywood, what bothered you the most about it?
A: I think there are really two types of acting. The professional way is to work in Hollywood, on TV, or in Paris, and to take a script and do the best work they can, trying to make things believable within the confines of what they've given you. The other way is a creative interpretation that, without caring about your career or money, tries to clarify a life through the expression of feelings and using intelligence. Even though that's not necessarily any longer connected to film, it's important to find oneself in the character. Too many actors lead a fashionable life. They make millions of dollars without really knowing why, listening to the advice of others and paying for an expensive house, taking roles and becoming businessmen and no longer being artists.

Some Hollywood directors are my friends, like Bob Aldrich, and I respect their work, but I can't work as an actor for just anyone anymore. I don't trust it, and even with a filmmaker I respect, I'm afraid that we'd say we were patronizing each other. I'd only work for Kazan and I think he would say the same thing. He's a terrific artist and I think that we consider each other as actors. But the others think of me as a director and that creates a difficult situation.

All decent actors are lunatics, difficult to live with. They fight over their lines, and it's good that's the case. For an actor, you don't want someone polite or tame. You want someone who's going to get angry. It's normal for someone to call me up at five o'clock in the morning to insult me. If someone is angry with me, I'm not going to say to myself that I'm not going to work with him under the pretext that they're giving me too much trouble. Instead, life is about living with problems, being a part of them. Sometimes I give direction that's completely off and the actor follows me blindly and it's a shame. But I don't have the right to force them to act badly. It's difficult to admit when it's my fault but at the same time I can't give someone the feeling of being thwarted. In front of a fifty-person crew, I'm always in the position of being right, and it's easy to blame the actor and heap abuse on them. But then I only destroy them, make them into an enemy and kill their dreams but also our own. In the process of defending myself I hurt myself. And I never liked directors because I always feel that's the attitude they adopt. All the actors I've known have problems. Once in a while, you meet directors who really like actors and make an effort to understand them. Very often in a professional film, they take you aside, they powder your face, they do your hair, they dress you, and when you find yourself back on the set you don't know where you are nor what to do. You want to speak with the director but it's the assistant who comes toward you saying, "Sit here, it's not your turn." So you're humiliated, your confidence is shot, you start to shake, you're going to be terrible, you're going to die. If you're an actor, you should never accept being put in this situation. If you came to see me, I would never tell you that you're going to have a wonderful time. And I wouldn't give you twenty pages of a script to read. What would you do? The night before you would drive yourself crazy trying to learn it. No, I'd tell you to come in tomorrow to act in a scene but while waiting I'd have a conversation with you, I'd try to make a friend out of you, not just to make you feel comfortable, but to relate to you as I would with a well-known actor. And I would certainly never ask you how you pour a glass of water or how you drink an orange juice, because how could someone "make believe" doing that? And neither would I give you directions for any such instruction by indicating specific gestures to you. It's absurd, it's limiting. No, what's necessary is mutual understanding and an understanding of human problems. Anyone knows how to sit, or drink naturally, if you're not forced to do things that don't feel true.

John Cassavetes in Los Angeles

Laurence Gavron / 1978

From *Positif,* April 1978. Reprinted by permission.

1. From *The Killing of a Chinese Bookie* to *Opening Night*

Sunset Boulevard nightclubs, cards, crooks, and sudden carnage—such is the world Cassavetes exhibits in *The Killing of a Chinese Bookie* (French Title: *Le Bal des Vauriens*). It's an underground world of shadow, this American underworld which has inspired so many filmmakers. But this film is not a thriller, and it's very different from what we might have expected. The script offers few surprises, and the characters matter more than the action. The plot is merely a pretext employed to look closely at the idiosyncrasies and organization of a unique society, to describe the speech and manners of its people, and above all to portray a particular character's dreams, decline, and collapse.

Manager of a Hollywood strip club, Cosmo Vitelli (Ben Gazzara) is neither a gangster nor a hero, just an ordinary man without much personality. Nonetheless he's ready for action when it comes to defending what's his. And his world is his club—the Crazy Horse West—where he has invested all his dreams and ambitions. A place of music, color, alcohol, and women, this neon universe comes alive through Cassavetes's camerawork, sensitively revealed via the power of visual suggestion. Locked away within the confines of his Never Never Land, Cosmo refuses to see the outside world for the real dangers it poses, and can't see his own death staring him in the face until it's too late.

From beginning to end, the camera follows this character, picking up the thoughts, emotions, and fears that lie behind his face and expressions, and capturing the relationships he's fostered with the women and patrons of his club in his role as master of ceremonies. All the action is condensed down to several hours, which is as long as it takes for Cosmo to finish his journey to the end of the Hollywood night. Since it has embraced the tempo of real time, the rhythm of the film seems quite slow, and the plot shows little concern for action and suspense. We're following the character through his daily life with simplicity and authenticity, just as we followed the couple in *Faces* and, as we did over barely two days, the three "heroes" of *Husbands*.

It's not until the middle of the film that the rhythm accelerates along with the action, which kicks into a higher gear when Cosmo sets off to perform a murder in exchange for settling a gambling debt. His itinerary follows the topography of his city—Los Angeles. After he leaves his world of nightclubs, poker, neon, and billboards, he passes by abandoned factories, deserted highways, and darkened streets into the heart of Chinatown and the sumptuous palace of the Chinese bookie himself. At the end of his nightmare, Cosmo finishes his task with a violence both brutal and effective. The scene of the kill, which happens suddenly, is one of the great moments of the film.

Via the naturalism of his camera movements, the expressive acting of the cast (nearly all used to his direction), the realistic length of the film, and the emotion he draws from his scenes and characters, Cassavetes demonstrates that his first priority is to describe, from within the allegory of the film, the atmosphere of social interaction and the roles of those who participate. Cosmo's voyage is a race between love and violence, between entertainment and crime, spectacle and death.

Opening Night, like *Woman Under the Influence*, is a film centered around a woman. Just like Mabel Longhetti in *A Woman Under the Influence*, Myrtle Gordon (also played by Gena Rowlands) sees her feelings, life, and dreams called into question. A woman: Who is she? What does she want, what should she do? John Cassavetes shows us that the subject is still under investigation, and that he still keeps this theme close to his heart.

Yet Mabel and Myrtle are opposites as well; two extreme cases of two very different women. Whereas Mabel was a housewife, a spouse and mother above all, who claimed that she had done nothing worthwhile in her life except her children, Myrtle is an actress for whom the only things that count are her career, the public, and the stage. A single woman without any kids, she has no real private life. Her entire world is her job: the stage, the parts she plays, and going on tour. Although she has relationships with others in the cast—with the writer of the play (Joan Blondell), the director (Ben Gazzara), the producer (Paul Stewart), and the other actors (among whom we recognize John Cassavetes himself)—her true happiness is the public, the applause, and the autographs.

Love was the center of Mabel's existence, whereas Myrtle's gravitates around the theater. She is totally obsessed by her art, her purpose—to create characters with whom audiences can identify. Her crisis erupts when in mid-career, she suddenly panics when she perceives the strange similarity between herself and the character of Virginia, a role she must perform in a play called "The Second Woman." Her own insecurities have been invisible to her up until this particular moment in her career when she must inhabit the role of a character that brings them out in her. And no one understands what's happening to her, starting with the author of the play, who seeks to impose her own interpretation on what it means to be a woman in the process of aging.

Myrtle finds herself incapable of inhabiting the role of Virginia because she doesn't feel the authenticity of the character, she doesn't understand the reactions of the woman, her problems, or her lack of humor. The uncomprehending reactions of those around her cause her, despite herself, to think she has herself changed, and grown older. And she "recreates" her youth via a fantasy—she hallucinates the presence of a young girl, Nancy, who adored her and who died in an accident at the back entrance of the theater. Thus, much like Virginia, Myrtle can't prevent looking back on her life, reconsidering her choices and questioning her career.

Opening Night, like Cassavetes's earlier films, examines characters through their physical expressions, their feelings and emotions, their interactions with others, and behavior when they are alone. The camera, both intimate and mobile, is an ever-vigilant witness to this central character. As is often the case with Cassavetes, action is restricted to just a few locations, closed spaces where the protagonists find themselves alone with or confronted by each other—on the stage, in the wings, or in hotel rooms. Exterior settings are few and brief, but powerful—for example, the magnificent shot with Myrtle alone in the crowd of New Yorkers, drunk and in anguish, yet resolved to fight on. The character is all the more moving since she is played, with matchless strength and sensitivity, by Gena Rowlands.

The script is perhaps more complex than usual, involving several elements, with emotion the most important theatrical characteristic. One might say the point of view of this film is more "neutral," more external. Beyond the characters, however, Cassavetes's eye is trained upon a theatrical universe and its world of actors. By his own admission, *Opening Night* is Cassavetes's favorite film, because, as he puts it, Myrtle Gordon is his favorite woman.

2. Interview

Q: Do you prefer Los Angeles, or do you miss New York?
A: I miss New York a great deal, I like that city a lot. For many years, I thought I would go crazy here. But I spend 80 percent of my life working, and the rest of the time with my family. So I don't notice the difference anymore.

Q: Is it easy for you to work here?
A: Yes, it's easier because there are no distractions, nothing I want to do here. It's as if I was on a desert island. It's better that way; in New York, the telephone is

always ringing, I want to see friends, go out, etc. I want to have a life, you know? Making films is a substitute for that.

Q: Do you mean therefore that you're not really living, you're only making films?
A: Yes, that's it! But I like it that way.

Q: When watching your films, the pleasure you take in making them is palpable. I get the feeling that you have a deep love for the actors, the camera, and the film itself.
A: It's because we all work together. Everyone who works on the film has the same stature, there isn't any hierarchy.

Q: Tell us about the film you just finished, *Opening Night*.
A: The music is very important in that film. Since it's a "female" film, it's about a working woman (Gena Rowlands), an actress, and her dreams and fantasies which she confuses with reality. And suddenly, someone tries to put an end to these dreams after so many years, telling her: "You don't like this play because you're starting to grow old." She doesn't consider for a single second that this reasoning is legitimate, but she's unable to disprove it. And throughout the film, she is going to struggle alone, saying "If I accept this, I'm screwed, it's over; I can't have any more joy, any more pleasure. . . ." So she fights, and ultimately she wins.

Q: Do you prefer to work as an actor or a director?
A: I don't care. If one becomes a filmmaker, you start to think of yourself first and foremost as a filmmaker, to take yourself seriously. I don't like these labels.

Q: Do you want to say, for example, that certain people who make films want to "be filmmakers" for the social status, when I think you are motivated above all by the desire to make films?
A: I love to tell a story. When you know ahead of time what the story is going to be, it's not fun anymore, it quickly becomes annoying. When I make a film, it's worthwhile to take a difficult subject and deepen it, and see if, in making a film on this subject, you can find something in yourself, and if others can find something in themselves that they can develop in their personal lives. And that's really great.

For *Opening Night* I had a wonderful story that came to mind, the story of this woman, Myrtle Gordon. What's unique about the woman in my film is that she is totally honest with herself, very persistent, and fundamentally alone. At times I think about her, I imagine her in the process of struggling, and I say to myself: "Oh, why can't she just be happy being a woman? How come she can't stop questioning herself so stubbornly, and always only seeing one side of things? If only she had a sense of humor!" I think: "Just be a woman, and that's final! Enjoy life, have fun, find a man, spend the night together. . . . Do something, for God's sake!" But she clings to what makes her happy, despite all the hostility around her. And that's also what makes her so unique—she sticks to it and ultimately she wins the case, even though there's no real "case" in life. In fact, she doesn't win anything at all, she only manages to obtain that which makes her happy. And for me, that's what it's all about.

Q: *The Killing of a Chinese Bookie*, your previous film, hasn't been shown in France yet, and has been rather poorly received here, by the public as well as critics. How do you explain this?
A: No one likes the film, other than two or three American critics; all the others trashed it. In one way, out of all my films, it's the one I care about the most; when there's a child that no one loves, the parents are going to love that kid all the more!

The film came out this summer in Canada, after being shown at the Montreal Film Festival. It was very well-received. Before it was shown, no one wanted the film in Canada, afterwards, they all wanted it! Everyone who hated it now wants to see it again!

The film was sold in France. It should be shown at the Paris Film Festival, and then be released after that; I don't know exactly what happened.

Q: For how long did you work on *Opening Night*?
A: I don't remember exactly when I started to write the screenplay. It actually took several years to finish, a month here and a month there. It's been about a year from when I finished the screenplay to today; the film should come out next month. [The film was released in Los Angeles on December 22, 1977.]

When you feel that the film is almost done, that's my favorite moment, it's so exciting! The shooting really drags on; as for the editing, it's suicide. You find yourself confronting so many disappointments—this doesn't work like I thought it would, this actor isn't happy . . . and you have to keep going, continue no matter what. And you think that the film will never get any better; you say to yourself "What is this thing I'm working on? It's meaningless, it doesn't work at all. . . ." Then suddenly you do something you like, then another, and the film starts to improve. And then all at once the film starts to take shape and that's when things start coming together quickly.

Q: When you write a script, do you start with a story, characters, or feelings . . . or is it that you know in your head already what the film is about, and have specific ideas as far as the way you want the story to be filmed?
A: No. Usually I start from a premise, a basic idea. For example, *Opening Night*

deals with how people react to growing old; how do you "succeed" when you're not wanted or desired as much as before, when you don't have as much confidence in yourself, in your potential, when you have less energy than before . . . and how do you become aware of it? That's the primary subject of the film. The second is to show the life of an artist, a creator. I think I know what the life of someone who creates is like. But for an actor, it's different.

Q: But you're both actor and creator at the same time.

A: Yes. And the actor is what interests me the most. Because actors don't have anything else to offer other than themselves, and their way of communicating is so special and different, that if something intervenes, it's impossible to express the shock to their spirit, their feelings, the way they are wounded by it. They can get a grip on themselves, but the wound is important, it impacts their personality, their way of life, their philosophy.

All this interests me a lot. So I thought this would be a wonderful character—a woman without the usual weapons, the typical habits women have: tears, sentiment, gentleness, all the usual stuff. Instead, take a woman with a career, a profession. Of course, she's not interested in children, nor men. However, she's a character with feelings. But she has a job to do, a career to pursue, and that's the most important thing for her. And in this case, her job is to be an actress.

So from this beginning, different ideas took shape progressively, and I started to write the script. I made a first draft, then a second, and so on. Then, once the actors were chosen, they started to tell me "I don't like this or that" and "I don't want to just be functional, be merely a character." But very quickly they realize that everything in their character is conventional, because they're part of a story. People who want to succeed, want to be right, want to be understood—they're all conventional. And actors are generally people who don't care if they're wrong or right. Because their only problem is communicating a specific thought in a way that's clearly understood. And this is difficult work. Therefore, they want to know why your feelings are different from theirs. And if you don't tell them, they attack you. And this woman can't defend against these attacks that come not from enemies, but from friends. These assaults are much more dangerous because they can shatter her self-image, or what she is trying to accomplish, much more rapidly. It's easy to say, "This idiot doesn't know what they're talking about," but if it's someone you know and respect, then it hurts to hear you're wrong. And when Myrtle hears these attacks, she can't work as she usually does because she's no longer sure she's right. Because her feelings are fragile, they don't come from a magazine, or Women's Lib, or from talking with her husband, or whatever. She thinks for herself; she's brave to try out her own personal ideals.

Q: In the film, did you draw from realistic elements, things known personally to you, Gena Rowlands, Ben Gazzara, or others around you?

A: In a way. I didn't consider Gena's opinion, Ben's opinion, or my own, as an actor. Because I'm more "romantic" as an actor than when I direct or when I write. When I act, I "romanticize" everything because I know it works. I know that the audience wants to laugh, they want everything to feel accurate, so my job as an actor is to make things clear for the audience.

As far as the ideas that are in the film, yes, they came to me from all the people I know. Not their "opinions" but what I see is really in their character. And I've often seen my wife try to express a feeling, an idea, something, or also my children, or myself. . . .

For example, I've always seemed young. And suddenly, I'm going to be forty-eight; I look at myself in the mirror sometimes and I say, "What's this stupid face all about? Who would want such a face?" So I understand these sorts of feelings. All the more because I'm not particularly vain. So imagine someone with this level of vanity, someone who was told by everyone that they were exactly what they seemed to be, were merely who they looked like, not who they really were. So no one really knows you, sees inside of you. And real communication from one soul to another is so rare, and only lasts a moment, even with those you're closest to. Everything else is rather superficial, and that's what makes up our lives. So it's difficult to identify that, to dig into it and make a film out of it. Also, no one thought it would be easy. We thought everything might fail because it was an ambitious project. But this made things all the more exciting. When we started to feel a certain emotion, to understand a scene, to believe in it . . . then the film started to work. It comes from a certain "comfort" with the process, when you get used to the characters. I don't think there is a director, a writer, or an actor alive who knows what uniquely makes a scene. What's unique is difficult to recognize. It's a secret within the heart, and none of us knows it.

All one can do is work hard enough to succeed; if one fails, it's hard! But it's good to be able to say, "I did that. I didn't try to take care of other people's lives as much as I did my own." That's all.

So, based on what I just said, to respond to your question after going off on a long tangent, yes, everyone contributes, but they do it in an ordinary way. Not by saying, "This woman is getting older, therefore that's a problem for her, she's an old woman . . ."; it's completely the opposite. Our task is how to give other women the freedom to think they're not old merely because someone tells them so. How do you ensure that they believe that, by the end of the film, and not simply by making a statement. And that's exciting.

Q: It's interesting that within the film, there is the constant presence of the theater, the stage. Would you like to put on a play?

A: I've never really liked theater, at least not as much as some. I respect the theater and the people who are a part of it, and I think it's wonderful for an actor. But it so happens I love film! I think of it as being something close to what I love. Theater is a fantastic intellectual exercise, which isn't put to good use often enough. There aren't many plays I like, and the plays I like are never emotional enough. They don't express half as much as what I like to see expressed. So I'm not happy with them. While film, by its very nature, allows for more imagination. Because a movie isn't life, it's just a reel of film! That's why a film always has to try very hard to be extremely "real," in order for us to react in a vocal way, laugh or cry . . . we have to participate in it, involve ourselves, and we can't notice any falsehoods. While in the theater an actor can really present himself grandly because it's larger than life, there is a significant difference there.

The audience wants to laugh much more, or cry . . . they're usually ready to cry. When watching films, they're more demanding, they want to be distracted. That's why it's a miracle if you manage to express something in a film. Because the public accepts practically everything that is easy, expected, and moves quickly! In fact it hates ideas. If you say a film is filled with ideas, no one will go see it!

Q: What do you think of today's young American filmmakers?

A: Among those I know personally, I think today's young filmmakers are trying to be as good as their elders. They have the same potential, but I don't think they have the same nerve. Without good writing, I don't think they would be as successful. Because with respect to technique, we've seen everything there is, and after a while, they're not so important any more. The same techniques have been more and more perfected—I mean, what more can you do with a camera? It's not enough. You can scrutinize yourself, that's been done. We've done everything we can to analyze everything mechanically. But then, what's really difficult? What about responding to questions about life, our sense of belonging, our solitude, our love, our happiness, our joys?

Q: Simple and authentic feelings?

A: Exactly. And I think young filmmakers are grasping this more and more, but some people aren't going to grasp it at once.

When you make your first film, it's a labor of love, which gathers up all the emotions you've ever known. Then the second film isn't as good, the third is a little better than that, and with the fourth, it's become a job. By the fifth film you're aware of all your mistakes. At a certain point, you start to understand that you can't work only for success, for the reviews, or for "art," but you have to do something substantial with your life, study life and develop your own style, a way to express yourself personally about what bothers you, what you like, or whatever. . . . And I think that young filmmakers will have a greater potential in this regard in about ten years.

Peckinpah was terrific, he had lots of talent, but he didn't have the right atmosphere to work in. He was totally destitute because of all the lawyers, accountants, bankers, and businessmen . . . all these horrible people. At the same time, Peckinpah would be equally horrible in their eyes if he walked into their offices and tried to run their businesses.

It's because of this that people "die." I don't want to say that Peckinpah's dead, but his talent suffered. Because he suffered from it. It's the same thing with Altman. Although Altman still does good work, and Peckinpah also, they are constantly on the defensive with respect to those who supervise them. So of course they aren't in a position to produce the best they have to offer. They're not really free because they're always on the defensive. A film "must" be a success, so suddenly they find themselves in competition with the major studios.

I have the same problem. In one way or another, my film has to work, or else I won't ever be able to make another one. But all the same, I accept that I am not in competition with the majors. Their film could be good, but it has nothing to do with mine. We have our world that belongs to us, and we believe in it, and we don't want the whole world to join us. And neither do we want everyone against us. We simply just want the chance to make what we make. It's important that young people at least know they have the choice. What difference does it make if they become "commercial" or "artistic"? Every time an artist becomes commercial, it restores balance. When an artist fails, of course it's hard to accept, because there are so few artists. We get angry because they accomplished a "superhuman" task, and society tells them they're wrong. And the public tells them they're wrong. However, it's difficult to tell them: "Keep going for a hundred years, until your death, until you're an old stupid guy that no one likes, who everyone makes fun of."

Q: *Opening Night*, like *Chinese Bookie* and *A Woman Under the Influence*, were both made independently. Would you ever consider eventually making films again for a studio?
A: Yes, right away! I'm okay with it because for me, a studio just means money. I'd do it all: act, direct, write.

Q: Wouldn't that mean you would have to make concessions?
A: If that implied concessions, then I wouldn't do it! I suffer like everyone else. I know that what I do makes me happy, but it's hard. It's hard to find money and

the time I need, it's hard when people think you're rich when you're not. It's hard to need money from everyone, constantly. . . . It's hard for my family. I'm pretty sure I'll never be rich because I've already spent more money than I'll ever make!

Sometimes I wonder what I'm making, I tell myself I could work for the studios, as an actor, scriptwriter, or director. I could listen to them, obey them, and take their money, like everyone else. Ultimately it's not that I'm proud of my work. I really appreciate the experiences, when I remember them . . . not the films, the adventures. Working with people who share everything, the ups and downs, whether they want it or not, they're pure, because they get nothing by way of compensation. And the film has to be good, or else they're unhappy.

Q: Your films are unique in a certain way, your style different from most other filmmakers. It's difficult to make comparisons, to speak of influences. . . .
A: Yes, and at the beginning, that annoyed me. I think that's the reason most people don't make original films, because it's uncomfortable. Equally, a musician is bothered if his music isn't compared to that of the great composers. In the same way, my films aren't comparable to those of the great directors.

And me, I've experienced all these anxieties. Audiences that walk out, leave the theater. And I think I don't give a damn. If everyone is happy, the film is good, I know that we have something. It's a strength, and it's not superficial or fleeting. I know that this is what people really want, because it's so powerful. What's better in life than worthy drama? It's something everyone understands, and the rest is foolishness. It's how you say things that matters, not what they say. That's the way to look at it, that's how to approach it.

And it's through our relationships, our friendships, our arguments, our discussions, all the "impersonal" feelings we have in relation to work, all that makes it exciting, because we all love this work enormously. And we know that no one's lying, that everyone's trying to get better, so everyone's giving all they have to give, this is the type of relationship we have.

For example, I don't like editing, but I have to be there next to the editor, because if I wasn't there, it would mean I didn't care about the film. I know that. And I hate it, I've always hated editing, because it's a manipulation that hurts people. Sometimes an actor has a great scene and I'm not paying enough attention to notice, or I see it but I'm thinking about my story. So I'm not afraid to make a decision, because I usually prioritize the actor over the story, but the editor doesn't have the same outlook, he doesn't have the same attachment that I have to the actors, so he can do a better job, he will have a better judgment.

I'm still very involved. For example, there was this great shot of Gena before and after the credits, and I took it out. But I needed seven months to make up my mind to take it out. Because I thought it was superfluous, something that might confuse the audience. But I loved that shot so much! I loved that moment, for the actor.

Q: Do you use a lot of film, in order to have more choices in editing?
A: Yes, totally.

Q: Is it difficult then, since you have to leave out a certain number of scenes and shots that you would have perhaps liked to keep, vis-à-vis the actors, for example?
A: No, it's not really hard for me since I've always worked that way, and I'm used to it. Having lots of different takes gives you lots of different ideas. And I really discuss these ideas with the actors. The actors are invited to all the showings, and there are loads of them, throughout which the film changes considerably. An actor will say, "I was terrible," and I will listen to him, I will ask him why. "Because I think the film . . ." but I don't want to hear about the film, I want to know what the actors think of themselves, what they didn't like about their performance. Because, let's be honest, that's what matters for them and not the goddamn film!
   So I always consider their opinion, and depending on what they tell me, I'll make changes in editing. Often, they'll have specific ideas about their character. As I change the film, I try to give them what they were missing.

Q: Do you only ask the actors' opinions, or do you also ask the rest of the crew?
A: I never ask the crew's advice. I don't think they're pure, purely interested in the emotions. For me, the actors are the fundamental creative force, because if their approach, their understanding of the issue is good, the film succeeds, and the work of the technical team is ultimately secondary. I admire and like people who work behind the camera, but they want to do a good job, nothing more. They wouldn't be happy if their work was poor, but they completely don't care about the story. Their main task is to execute their part of the job well. While for the actors the story is important since their character is reflected in the overall story. If Ben Gazzara doesn't feel involved in the story, even if he's great, he knows the audience won't be interested, won't pay attention . . . of course he wants the film to be a success.

Q: It's your third film, after *Husbands* and *Minnie and Moskowitz*, where you direct yourself. . . .
A: Yes, and all three times were very different. I had a lot of fun with this film, *Opening Night*, because I didn't have to learn anything, because I know how to be an actor. And my character is just an actor, neither good nor bad, simply an actor.

Someone who's trying to make a living. I liked that. Each time I came on set I had a great time with it. And I could let myself become this character totally without thinking of anyone else.

With *Husbands*, I loved the two men I was with, Ben Gazzara and Peter Falk, who are the two best actors I know, and I loved all the other characters. . . . And there was no director for that film, so I had to do the direction! So I was simultaneously inside and out; sometimes on the inside of the film, sometimes outside.

Cassavetes on Cassavetes

Monthly Film Bulletin / 1978

From *Monthly Film Bulletin*, June 1978. Reprinted by permission of the British Film Institute.

(Extracts from an interview with John Cassavetes conducted soon after the release of *Opening Night* in the United States.)

I think it's an enormous struggle to make films, wearing, unromantic. I used to make films, *Shadows* and *Faces*, on the basis of intelligence, where I'd go out to work and over a three or four year period complete a film. Then I realized at one point that I had spent seven years in an editing room on two films, and I thought there must be some better approach to it. I got smarter, and just found a way to raise the money and to complete it. But maybe that was a mistake. This film [*Opening Night*] cost about a million and a half, which I borrowed, and it's just been a terrible experience. The financial conditions were impossible. So much so that I really have absolutely no feeling for the picture itself. Every film is an experience and really relates back to the way you worked on it, what kind of a pleasure it was in dealing with the people. This was just a war from the beginning, to see if we could do it; I found myself spending all my energy saying, I don't care, we'll do it anyway.

A Woman Under the Influence was enormously successful, but what you have to spend to make it is terrifying. I thought *Woman* was an absolutely wonderful movie, and I could watch it many times, except that it's so painful I can't watch it. I saw some girls, and they had come from San Francisco to see the film, and they said we loved *Woman*, and when Peter Falk went up to San Francisco we booed him. Now we saw the picture again and we thought he was the most romantic figure that ever existed, because he really cared about that woman enough to make mistakes. Here is a man who has an incredible wife, whom he really doesn't want to share with anyone, because she stirs his imagination, she is outspoken. She's everything that he wants, physically, spiritually, mentally, but he's ashamed, because she doesn't conform. Well, she couldn't entice him if she conformed, and so he double-crosses her, when it becomes a pain in the ass to him. He falls out of love with her, momentarily, it becomes too much, he's out of the mood. I thought that the wonderful thing about the picture, apart from the children, who were really good, was that we had taken away the pettiness of women as a weapon. The woman in a sense became idealized; you took the purity of a woman minus pettiness, and you took a totally real character, whom Peter Falk played, totally in love with a woman, subject to the new moralities and the New Woman, and he was trying to do the best he could.

We did *The Killing of a Chinese Bookie* just as an effort to get out of the distribution business. We started writing it two weeks before we started shooting. Years ago, Martin Scorsese and I were talking, and in one night made up this gangster story. Years later, when I didn't know what to make, I thought we'll do that story about this nightclub owner who owes a lot of money, and is talked into killing someone who isn't really the person he thinks he's going to be killing. But mainly it was about a conformist, about somebody who would have been a white-collar worker years ago, and who does all the right things and who is going to be killed for it. I think that's mainly why the audience couldn't identify with him. I remember very distinctly when we were shooting the scene in which he lost all the money, and then he went and shook the hands of the criminals. And Ben Gazzara did it with such skill and sincerity. I kept thinking, if we do this another twenty times, maybe Ben will reach the audience by enjoying it more. I thought the difference between success and failure, in terms of the audience response, would have been had he said, thank you very much! instead of thank you, thank you. I thought that little point would either make the audience go with him as a character or say I want to shy away from him, because he really is polite, he's not putting anyone down, he's not standing up for himself. I think it became a sad film for most people, because that point of reality was something they couldn't swallow. I'd like to make that film about four or five more times, because it had interesting characters, interesting people.

Opening Night I thought was an enjoyable movie. It wasn't supposed to be anything superb; it's about theatre, it's not the end of your life. Most of the people who like the film are touched by the discussion of age, yet it's really not about age. It's one of the problems that actors, or theatre people, discuss. Mainly I think her resentment is deep and very universal, it's about being pigeonholed. She didn't have any problem with age when she began that play. I think that her problem was that she felt she didn't have anything individual to say about this particular subject. She didn't have any feeling about it. Then she got to have feeling about it, because it was written by an older woman, who challenged her and said, you're old too, you understand, and pigeonholed her into being in her own group.

The film had two selves. And one was that background of Gena Rowlands's own personal life, of children, family, home, schooling; the problems of who you are and trying to fight for your own individual survival as you do all these other prescribed chores. But this selfish, individual part of the person, your own mind's-eye-view of yourself, is to me the epitome of an actress. It's what you could be if none of these other things existed. If you would have no boundaries of commitment. You could then express so much. But in one sense, to me, it's an anti-art film, in that it says, if you had your way, you wouldn't express a goddamn thing. If you had your total way. Actors, or writers, have to work under this duress—under a limited duress, you can't be tortured, your ears can't be torn off, your moustache pulled out hair by hair.

The three generations of women were important, because I think that, while it's masculinely directed and presented, the film really is about women and their points of view as professionals. Here's an old lady, Joan Blondell, who still has all her life and sexual feelings, which you can see though we don't go into them; and Gena, who's a few decades down from Joan, and the young girl, who is really seventeen years old. And these three generations do haunt the waking hours of women: your powers waning, your attractiveness having to be worked on more. I think these are real things, and to put them in terms of this story really gave me fits. Here's a theatrical story, and suddenly this apparition appears—and I started giggling. Everybody knows I hate that spooky-dooky stuff, and they said, are you going to leave that in? But this is a figment of her imagination, it's not a fantasy, it's something that's controllable by her. It's something necessitated by her own loneliness and individuality, and she's childlike, by the very nature of being an actress. And it isn't a man. A man wouldn't have that apparition; he'd dream of a dead body or his own demise.

I really think that every character in this is a cliché, with the exception of Gena, because all of us are clichés, and we can all be deciphered once somebody knows us. The artist is really a magical figure, whom we would all like to be like and don't have the courage to be, because we don't have the strength to be obsessive. Gena had the most difficult part, because it was the least defined and the least connected with other people. I said, we're going to take it objectively; it's not going to be a subjective point of view which people can identify with quite easily, because I don't think they want to identify with performers, backstage theatricality, to the point where they become just as mundane as everybody else. So we shot it much more conventionally, and we didn't use those strengths that we know can create loneliness: long shot, then tight shot, key lighting and everything else. Everything was normally lit by Al Ruban, and nothing was really explained. She came in drunk, we didn't know quite why she'd decided to drink; we didn't know quite why she smoked a lot of cigarettes; we didn't know quite why she didn't like the play. It was never articulated that clearly, yet it was all there for people to see as themselves if they were that actress.

You never see her as a stupendous actress. As a matter of fact, her greatest thrill was comfort, as it is for most actresses. Give me a play I can go into every night and can feel I have some awareness of who I am, what I am. There are other parts where you play people who you know people are not going to like. They're not going to like somebody who complains about their life when they have no complaint. So an actor is street smart, and Gena as Myrtle Gordon was street smart; she said, I don't like the role, it's not going to be sympathetic, I don't want to expose myself in those areas. So when she faints and screams on the stage, it's because it's so impossible to be told you are this boring character, you are ageing and you are just like her. I would be unable to go on to the stage feeling that I'm nothing. I think that most actors would, and that's really what the picture is about.

Talk Show

Colin Dangaard / 1978

From *New York Sunday News*, June 11, 1978. © Daily News, L.P. (New York). Used with permission.

Guest: John Cassavetes
Talking about: his wife (actress Gena Rowlands)

One reason I became a director and started making my own films was that I wanted to keep my family together. It was not so much that I wanted to make films, as I wanted to make films around the people with whom I want to spend my life.

I really married the woman I like. I haven't changed my feelings over the years, and I don't believe she has changed hers either.

Not even I can find fault with Gena. I am a one-woman man and I like it that way. Oh, sure, there is an element of competition, with her acting as well. But the competition is fun, just like our fights.

We have found we have absolutely dissimilar tastes, in everything we think, do, and feel. We have also found love is not a constant stream. It diminishes. It's calm. It's dull. And then it gets exciting. If you hang in there, it gets very interesting.

I just don't think I could go on without my wife. I wouldn't want to live.

John Cassavetes Gets His Reward

Dolores Barclay / 1980

From *Los Angeles Times*, July 8, 1980. Used with permission of The Associated Press.

Sometimes, it's hard marching to the tune of a different drummer. Sometimes, it pays off.

Ask John Cassavetes, the independent filmmaker who's finally getting his due reward.

After two decades, American recognition has been bestowed on the fifty-year-old director-writer-actor. The Museum of Modern Art is running a retrospective of his works—under the same roof as the highly acclaimed Picasso exhibit. In March, Cassavetes was honored by Filmex in Los Angeles.

"You really do want a voluntary acknowledgement that you're an artist," he said in an interview. "When the museum started going through all of this stuff on opening night, I was kind of excited. I wasn't flattered, but I was happy."

"I'm so honored," grinned the hero of every would-be filmmaker, "because a scene from my first film was shot in the museum. I've always had a very soft spot for the place."

His first film was *Shadows*, filmed from 1957 to 1960 on what amounted to pennies, with a handheld 16mm camera. Technically, the film was a misfit, critics said. But as art, it's been called a masterpiece.

"The type of films we do are different," said Cassavetes, savoring a bottle of imported beer at a midtown restaurant. "Commercial movies have no feeling, no sensitivity. Most people tell me that people won't understand films with feeling. But everyone can feel."

Including Cassavetes, who remains unscathed by the criticism he must hear. "I get a little bugged by critics," he said. "Most give me great notices, and then rap me.

"By the age of fifty, I would like to know that I'm not dead—that there's some continuity to my life."

The maître d' in the restaurant was startled to see Cassavetes, who played opposite Mia Farrow in *Rosemary's Baby*. He dashed over to the artist, not for an autograph, but to tell him he must put on a tie.

Cassavetes threw back his head and laughed. An attendant brought the adornment and Cassavetes put it round his neck, looped it like an ascot, and laughed again.

"Look," he said, leaning across the table. "I think people are very stiff. Money makes people stiff and we want it and we have to pay the penalty. I never agreed with the stiffness.

"I think people have an understanding of what their life is. I define success by being a realist and not humiliating people.

"I'm a revolutionary—but not in the political sense."

When he discusses his work, he speaks in terms of "we." Cassavetes is referring to the people with whom he constantly works to make his movies—his wife, Gena Rowlands, who stars in many of his works, and his friends actors Ben Gazzara and Peter Falk.

"I like what's best for me and my friends," he said, laughing. "I have no sense of responsibility and I'm proud of it. It's wonderful.

"If it came to a good film or what makes feeling, I'd take feeling."

Cassavetes is a native of much of New York.

"My father was a gambler—he gambled with us," he said. "We never knew what poverty was. We never knew we were poor when we were poor. We never knew we were rich when we were rich.

"But we were always in the kitchen."

He left the kitchen long enough to play a brooding young bullfighter in a production by the old *Omnibus* television series in 1953. That led to roles in *Playhouse 90*, *Studio One*, *Kraft Theater*, and *Climax*.

His official debut for the silver screen was in *The Night Holds Terror*.

Shadows was the result of an improvisation class Cassavetes taught. After its release, he entered it in the Venice Film Festival where it won five awards. Later, in 1963, *Faces* also captured five awards at the festival.

Cassavetes's *A Woman Under the Influence* with Rowlands and Falk won him an Oscar nomination for best director in 1974.

Rowlands now is filming *Gloria* with her husband. It is the story of an ex-gun moll and showgirl who suddenly is burdened with a seven-year-old boy after his family is murdered in a gangland hit.

Why *Gloria*?

"Look," said Cassavetes, "I'm not very bright. I wrote a very fast-moving, thoughtless piece about gangsters. And I don't even know any gangsters.

"*Gloria* has a wonderful actress and a very nice kid who's neither sympathetic nor nonsympathetic. He's just a kid.

"He reminds me of me, constantly in shock, reacting to this unfathomable environment."

Cassavetes: Making of a Movie Maker

Charles Schreger / 1980

From *Los Angeles Times*, September 16, 1980. Copyright © 1980 Los Angeles Times. Reprinted with Permission.

John Cassavetes on today's films:

"I always feel left out of most movies. They have nothing to do with me."

John Cassavetes on the impact of his films (*Shadows*, *Faces*, *Husbands*, *A Woman Under the Influence*) on cinema:

"I don't think films are the same as when we started out. We've made a difference."

John Cassavetes on his movies as art:

"I would put my pictures up against anybody's in this world. Certainly in my own day I bow to no one. I don't think there's another director in the world who works harder to make better films than I do."

And John Cassavetes on his movies and accessibility:

"That word bothers me, really. I don't think that people want their lives to be easy. I think it's a United States sickness. In the end it becomes more difficult. I like things to be difficult so that my life will be easier."

There you have it, a primer on director Cassavetes, depending on where you stand, a filmmaker who is complex, arrogant, self-assured, self-absorbed, para-doxical, emotional, perplexing, challenging, boring, self-indulgent, or brilliant.

Regardless, in the truest sense of the word, Cassavetes is an independent. He has been acting in films since the mid-1950s (*Edge of the City*, *The Dirty Dozen*) and directing them since 1961 with *Shadows*.

His work as a director has been alternately praised and scorned. His last film, *Opening Night*, was released in the United States in 1978—in one theater.

He has been independent in the sense that he works outside the studio system, finding his own financing and distribution.

But that has changed with his latest film, *Gloria*, an offbeat gangster film starring his wife Gena Rowlands. It opens next month, but already can be called a prize-winning film after taking home top honors at the recently completed Venice Film Festival.

Gloria was backed by Columbia Pictures, which wasn't bothered by Cassavetes's rather rocky commercial track record.

Was there much difference working at a studio rather than as an independent?

"There isn't too much difference, really," Cassavetes said recently. He was seated in a conference room at the Burbank Studios, part of the suite of offices lent to him by his friend and sometimes collaborator Peter Falk. Cassavetes was thoughtful and intense. He gives the impression, sometimes, that when he's staring at you he's staring through you.

Before going off to Toronto for ten weeks to act in a Canadian production, *Incubus*, Cassavetes agreed to sit and discuss his latest film, his recent award, American movie audiences, and other assorted concerns.

"At least with me when I work with a major company, it's still the same crew, the same actors, the same cameras. You just have a little bit more of everything," he said.

Perhaps one difference, as Cassavetes acknowledged, is that you come to the studio and its structure with a reputation, which can make life easier, or more difficult.

"Your reputation precedes you as this kind of neurotic man that doesn't have any script," he said. "The people at the studio have read the reviews of the pictures and they *know* that they're unstructured, that we just go and make it up as we go along.

"It would be really wonderful if we could do that. I'd really like to."

Winning the Golden Lion award for best picture at Venice is not Cassavetes's first recognition in that city or in Europe. Traditionally, his films have been well received in Europe, and he's won the Golden Lion before.

"It's a beautiful city, Venice, and they revel in beauty and art," he said. "Art is something that they acknowledge in their lives."

Implied, then, is that art is something American film audiences don't necessarily revel in.

"This country is built upon endorsements," Cassavetes added. His words are strong and harsh, but his tone of voice calm.

"If you watch television, if you read the newspapers, if you go to a movie, the first thing somebody asks is 'How many people were there? Was it crowded?' That's the nature of the success of a film in this country.

"I just feel that in Europe, that the person who makes the film is more highly regarded and there's more expected of that person to be original. Here, though, if you break the genre of the film, it's disturbing the public.

"In Europe, that's what they look for. You get points for originality there."

Anyone who has seen Cassavetes's films—and some like *Killing of a Chinese Bookie* and *Mikey and Nicky* are tough to find, while *Husbands* and *Minnie and Moskowitz* play on TV or in revival houses—will agree that they are original. Another important word is emotional.

"I contend that it's a difficult trick to make people feel emotion today," Cassavetes said. "Most people don't feel anything today because they've been so dumped on by a bunch of brandied, caked French cooking over life.

"I think that American audiences, more than anything, take time to adjust. If they can't fit a film into what they expected, it's hard for them to believe that there is something there that they don't know about.

"I make pictures not for the intelligentsia. We don't shoot through glasses. The films are straightforward."

Some might argue otherwise. Still, Cassavetes's movies are deliberate, there is an underlying structure and intention. To him, clearly they are art.

For Cassavetes there have been frustrations. But he has no regrets.

"If I had my artistic life to do over again, I don't think that I would be as lucky as I have been. Certainly I can look upon my life as not being wasted.

"People say to me, 'You're an iconoclastic kind of guy who just does this kind of thing. You're a maverick, an angry young man.'

"I'm not a young man, number one. I'm not angry at anyone, number two. And I'm not a maverick. I just like to make movies."

Cassavetes: "Show Me the Magic"

Michael Ventura / 1982

From *LA Weekly*, August 20–26, 1982. Reprinted by permission of Michael Ventura.

"Sonofabitch—what I wouldn't give for a different nightmare."
—Cassavetes playing Phillip in Paul Mazursky's *Tempest*

The people who did the trailers for Paul Mazursky's new film, *Tempest*, knew what they were doing: John Cassavetes, amidst flashes of lightning, saying with all the intensity at that intense man's command, "Show me the magic. Come on. *Come on*, show me the magic."

As actor, writer, and especially director, it has been the work of Cassavetes's life to show us the magic—and it has been the discipline of his life to look for that magic not in special effects that can only take place on movie-screens, or in the often easy outs of fantasies, but in the look on a woman's face between the time she puts her kids on the bus to school and the time she goes crazy; or the look on a man's face, after he's vomited in a bathroom in a bar, when he can look up from his humiliation into the eyes of a friend. It's the magic that happens when all the layers are peeled off, no defenses, no tricks—nothing but that great trickster, the human heart, quickened for a moment into honesty.

He is deeply committed in grounding his philosophic points in what he calls "real things"—"because," he told me, "I too am a member of this age—this age of nihilistic positivity, or whatever the hell it is."

The Age of Nihilistic Positivity—as good a name for our era as I've heard. For twenty years now his films have taken the side of those who must earn their baffled living in the Age of Nihilistic Positivity: *Shadows*, *Faces*, *Husbands*, *Minnie and Moskowitz*, *A Woman Under the Influence*, *The Killing of a Chinese Bookie*, *Gloria*. I've written elsewhere and at length about the tremendous influence of his direction, and how moments and filmic styles we take for granted in many films were first explored and given form in his. And as an actor, Cassavetes has stood for a style that can be popular without being homogeneous, without ironing out the natural quirks and flaws and fissures of the psyche.

In Mazurksy's *Tempest* he gives us his best performance in a decade, a fiery, funny, feisty portrait of a man who decides the only way to stay is to leave, the only way to safety is to risk everything, the only laughter worth laughing is the laugh that brings tears to your eyes.

Ventura: What was it like to work with Mazursky in *Tempest* as an actor?

Cassavetes: Well, when I first saw the script, my mind flashed back to all the incredible double-crosses people perform, particularly when they're working on an expensive picture. So the first thing I wanted was not to be double-crossed. And the only way you can not be double-crossed is to say up front what you feel. Straightforward. A lot of people thought the script was very good. I frankly didn't understand the script.

I understood that the guy was an architect and that he was having troubles with his wife and his way of life and job, and that's simple, that's everybody. It could be a workman just as easily as being an architect. But I didn't understand his reactions to the feeling that he was in—the change-of-life period, or whatever you want to call it. Somebody trying to be young, somebody trying to be vital the way they used to be. And finding himself in a position where everyone surrounding him is as dead as he is. And all the things you try to accomplish in your life suddenly come back on you and you realize you don't have that much time. So, when I read it, I didn't know if the struggle to get out of that was going to be handled honestly, movie-wise. I knew it was a comedy, because everyone said that. But I didn't know if Paul wanted me to do jokes, or act funny—which I can't do anyway—or if he'd let it be straight. And so I said, "I take this very seriously, this script."

I went into that meeting angry. And I didn't know why I was so angry, but I was angry. I think I wanted to let Paul know that there is a certain amount of bitterness that comes into the constant boredom of meeting people who don't connect with you—I mean, chemically, or just what they're doing. You get crazy, you just don't want to do it.

But Paul is very interesting. Because he's a man who doesn't really say a lot about what he's gonna do. He's always alive and vital and making statements that you can challenge. I mean, he's a dynamo! Dynamic man. Laughs in the middle of what actors would deem important scenes. And clowns around during rehearsals. And he prefers somebody to challenge his thoughts.

A lot of directors—not good ones—but a lot of directors let their script-girl tell them that you didn't say the line, that you left out a "But, I—" or something like that. You do a take over again. And the feeling is that it doesn't matter what's on the screen, it only matters that you left out a "But, I—." But with Paul—I very rarely work with a director, like him, who doesn't really challenge every specific comment, and yet watches every specific moment.

You know, sometimes everyone second-guesses the director. It's very simple to do and it's very normal. I'm sure when Mazursky acts he does the same thing. You know, you think, "My God, why do they have to push it in this direction, when it could be so lovely in *this* direction." That happens all the time. But Paul really likes that. He likes it in the sense that if you really know so much, *do* it. Don't sit and talk about it and conspire about it and fret about it. Put it on the screen. Who's stopping you?

And then he *might* stop you. But Paul's whole thing, not only in front of the camera, was a nice rapport between the actors.

And working with Paul wasn't, "This is the scene about the girl whom you meet for the first time," there's none of that. It's "Oh! There's Susan! [Susan Sarandon]. Gah! She looks great. Susan, you look great! Fantastic! Oh my God!" And Susan gets all embarrassed, she says, "Okay, Paul, let's do the scene," and he says, "Okay, the car is coming, *I'll* play the guy, I'll play the guy!" And off-scene Paul will play me, and he'll say, "There's no room for you, John, you get outta here!" And I found it, for everybody there, maddening, because it's a strange different kind of direction. But now I miss it. And I don't want to go back to the other.

I mean, he'd never say, "This is what it's about," "This is funny," "This is not." It's, "Look at that daughter, isn't she *wonderful*, God, she's better than you! She's better than Gena! She's better than anybody! God! She's marvelous!" Then he cries. Hugs her. Embraces her. Then you do the scene.

Or in Greece, in the Peloponnesus, he might storm into the bedroom and say, "Are you going to the party?! We have the boat tonight!" And Gena and I would be asleep. And he'd say, "I can only stay a minute, John. John, don't ask me what the dailies are like, I don't want to hear 'What are the dailies like'; don't ask me, you're gonna drive me crazy." "Would you like a drink, Paul?" "A drink?! No, I don't wanna drink, I toldja I can only stay a minute. Are you going to the party or not? Oh God, the dailies were really great, the dailies were . . ." and *then* he'd talk about them.

I've heard a lot of people talk about magic in films. I think, from my standpoint, that Paul was Phillip [the soul-searcher of *Tempest*], and so was I. But so was he. Not only *was* he, but then he insisted that the whole crew make magic! And if the weather turned and it was all just beautiful blue sky and *he* wanted it gray, then he'd go into the water and actually be doing these chants! So it was a delight.

Ventura: You said you walked into that first meeting angry?
Cassavetes: I think, like everybody, nobody trusts anybody. I'm not different.

And actors are particularly distrustful, and mean. Simply because they feel that no one is really going to be able to help them. Or be able to understand what the story is—that the author himself has written, but actors just feel that they know it. Your tendency as an actor is to create your own story immediately. Out of panic. And that's what happens in the beginning. And Paul just wanted that short period out.

Ventura: When you're directing, what's your approach to that period?

Cassavetes: I'm totally an intuitive person. I mean, I think about things that human beings would do, but I just am guessing—so I don't really have a preconceived vision of the way a performer should perform. Or, quote, the character, unquote. I don't believe in "the character." Once the actor's playing that part, *that's* the person. And it's up to that person to go in and do anything he can. If it takes the script this way and that, I let it do it. But that's because I really am more an actor than a director. And I appreciate that there might be some secrets in people. And that that might be more interesting than a "plot."

I like actors, and I depend on them a lot. I depend on them to think. And to be honest. And to say, "That never would happen to me, I don't believe it." And to try to decipher what is defense, and what is a real irregularity in somebody's behavioral pattern. And then I try to find some kind of positive way to make a world exist like a family—make a family, not of *us*, behind the camera, not of the actors but of the characters.

Ventura: A shared world?

Cassavetes: That they can patrol certain streets, patrol their house, and—that's what I feel people do, they know their way home. And when they cease to know the way home, things go wrong.

Ventura: How do you mean, know the way home?

Cassavetes: You somehow, drunk or sober or any other way, you always find your way back to where you live. And then you get detoured. And when you can't find your way home, that's when I consider it's worth it to make a film. 'Cause *that's* interesting. People are interested in people that are *really* in trouble. Not pretending to be.

Ventura: Did you discover that first as an actor?

Cassavetes: I think I discovered it on the streets. I think I discovered it in barrooms, when people talk about their life. And they're not worrying about paying a psychiatrist or worrying about the guy next to them. I think it's a given with men, or has been, that that's not just conversation, it's stating something else—so whatever somebody was talking about, they were talking about it for a reason. People in barrooms know that. Like being in a war, being in a bar.

And I think women probably—I don't know—I don't really know anything about women. I try to deal with women in films a lot differently than I would deal with men.

Ventura: How?
Cassavetes: I look at women much, much more fairly, because I'm not a woman. And I don't really know very much about them. So I try to make their life a little more straight-line, so that we won't be taking some opinionated view of a man taking an opinionated view of a woman—rather deal with it on a line of activity. Of what they do. And then their behavior comes out in their activity.

With men I don't do that. Because I feel I know men. I know men very well. I know all their hypocrisies, and the fact that they don't have babies, and how important that is, and what a pregnant woman means to a man, and what sports or non-sports mean, or philosophy, or culture, or when it happens, and when it's interesting to talk about, when it brings tears to the eyes, and when it means nothing. All the complexities of men I'm sure are like the complexities of women, but they're definitely in my opinion not the same. I don't care what the legislation says.

I still feel that women are more receptive by nature than a man is. I don't know whether it's a conditioning, or whatever—it's an actuality, anyway. I've seen my daughter, when she was very young, practice on me, practice seeing herself through a man's eyes. I mean, no one told her to do that. I don't see boys doing that. They don't practice being. They just grow up, and they are either something that pleases them, or nothing that pleases them. I don't think that the question of identity is so strong with a man as it is with a woman. It's just, most men don't go around worrying if they're good enough. And women do. And their whole life is a challenge.

Ventura: How did that view figure in *A Woman Under the Influence*?
Cassavetes: I only knew one thing about *Woman Under the Influence* when we started: that it was a difficult time for today's woman to be left alone while somebody goes out and—lives. And it's *fine* for a housewife to get her kids off to school. As irritating and annoying and boring as that may be, it's not the same as, later in the day, being totally alone with nothing to do, nothing you're supposed to do, except maybe darn a sock or something like that. So it becomes a very tough existence. So you look to get out. And what place do you have to go? Because when they all come back you're happy.

And I think that probably happens to every woman. I know when I was not working, and Gena was working for me—because I was really in trouble in this business, I'd done a lot of things where it really looked like I wasn't going to be able to work again—and I stayed home and took care of the baby, and I was a pretty good housewife and everything else, and I didn't have really much time to think about what was wrong and all, but I didn't have really the same reactions as a woman would have. Mainly because I didn't *have to* be a housewife the rest of my life. I didn't have to think into the future of when I'd get older or when my attractiveness would fade or when the kids would grow up or when the baby would cease to cling to you and you're not really a mother then and you have to think, well, should I be her friend or should I be the mother?

All those things are much more interesting than what they're making movies out of—taking a figure like Begelman. People are crazy, you know? They really are. Because they think that it's good enough to make a movie that you don't like, as long as it makes money. It's just much more interesting to find out whether you're going to live or die. Whether you're going to have a good time or not. Whether the children will be content with their life—not "content," but content with their *life*, you know? Not feel they have to be like everybody else.

Ventura: When you said you were in trouble with the industry, how were you in trouble?

Cassavetes: Well, I—I was young. And I felt that everybody had talent. And that for some reason they were being arbitrary and not employing that talent. 'Cause I thought, "Well, these people are the giants of an industry, they must have a good brain and a good heart and ability, how come they don't use it?" And Gena, she said, "Look, a lot of people just don't have the same drives, the same desires, the same gun that sparks them, as you do. You're acting like these people all understand you; nobody understands you. *I* don't understand you, who the hell can understand you?! You're nuts!"

But I would think *she* was crazy. And I would go in, and I would think, "Naw, this sonofabitch understands what I'm talking about—he just, for some reason, doesn't want to do it, I don't know what the hell it is with this guy." And I'd meet these people years later and we'd become friends and they'd say, "I don't know what the hell you were upset about!" But I'd go like a maniac. Because I figure, if you work on a picture, *that's your life*. For the moment. That you're working on a picture. It's like a beautiful woman. And you fall in love. And when the picture's over it's like a break-up of that love affair. And then somebody says, "Well, are you gonna do another picture," and it's offensive, because it's like saying, "When are you gonna fall in love again?"

I mean, *Husbands* was *Husbands*. I was in love with that picture, in love with Bennie [Ben Gazzara] and Peter [Peter Falk] and New York and London and hotel rooms and beautiful women and the whole adventure, behind the camera and in front of it, and it was one of the most romantic things that ever happened in my life. And *A Woman Under the Influence* was a wonderful experience—but it was hard.

Ventura: How?

Cassavetes: It was hard work. It was disciplined work. Something that made me feel good, the discipline, but it wasn't free-wheeling, you didn't feel like going out after the shooting. I usually like a lot of noise on the set. I didn't like any noise on *that* set. I felt the people who were doing it should be respected, because it's so embarrassing to relive moments that are private and delicate. And it was also not totally real. It was a concept. Of love. A concept of how much you have to pay for it.

That's kind of pretentious, but I was interested in it. And didn't know how to do it, and none of the other people knew how either, so we had to work extremely hard.

Ventura: You said it wasn't totally real? How would it have been?

Cassavetes: Well, it probably would have been nastier. I think in the whole picture the defensiveness was just removed. No one there is defensive in the whole film. There isn't one shield on anybody's psyche, or anybody's heart. It's just open. So you just have to work on a different level. You have to work on a higher level, and deal with philosophic points in terms of real things.

Ventura: How do you mean, in terms of real things?

Cassavetes: Real things. Children—are real. Food is real. A roof over your head is real. Taking the children to the bus is real. Trying to entertain them is real. Trying to find some way to be a good mother, a good wife, I think all those things are real. And they are usually interfered with by the other side of one's self—which is the personal side, not the profound, wonderful side of somebody's self. And that personal side says, "Hey, what about *me*? Yeah, you can do this to *me*, but, uh . . ." If you're in the audience, the audience is saying, "Hey, what about ME?" All the way through the picture, the characters are not—and therefore the audience is allowed to ask that, because the characters can't. So that was very difficult. And that's why it was unreal. Because in life people stop and say "What about me?" every three seconds.

Ventura: That accounts for the reaction that many women I know had to that picture, leaving it with this deep yet not bitter conviction that they had to change their situations NOW—the picture making them say "What about me?" for the character, and so for themselves.

Cassavetes: And Gena is the kind of person—I don't mean she's an actress—I mean, I'm sure she's an actress, but I don't see her that way: I see her as an incredibly gentle and kind person with this vision of what life could be.

I remember one time in the picture, when Gena was committed by Peter, and she went to an institution, and as the film says six months later she comes out—I would have thought that she would be so hostile against her husband. But she comes in the house and she never even acknowledges his presence. She's only considering her children. And we did a take, and I thought, "Should I stop this? I mean, she never looked at Peter." She walks in the house and everyone greets her and she never looks at her husband—I mean, she looks at him, but she never sees him, yet she's not avoiding him. And I thought, "Well, that's that defenseless thing carrying itself too far here, what are we doing?"

You know, ignorance is astounding, particularly when it's your own. And all through that homecoming scene I was astounded by what was underneath people, what these actors had gathered in the course of this movie. And I was *way* behind them. As a matter of fact, when we looked at the dailies, Gena said, "What do you think? I'm at a loss, did we go too far?" And I said, "I didn't like it, I just didn't like it at all." I mean, I found it really so embarrassing. To watch. It was such a horrible thing to do to somebody, to take her into a household with all those people after she'd been in an institution, and their inability to speak to this woman could put her right back in an institution, and yet they *were* speaking to her, and that Gena was so willing to get rid of them, and at the same time not insult them—but then I thought: what Gena did, it was like poetry. I thought the film really achieved something really remarkable *through the actors' performances, not giving way to situations but giving way to their personalities*. So it altered the narrative of the piece, but it really made it. I would grow to love those scenes very, very much, but the first time I didn't.

Ventura: When you say "altered the narrative," you mean—
Cassavetes: The dialogue was the same.

Ventura: But the *performances* changed the meaning of the scene—
Cassavetes: Sure.

Ventura: So because they didn't succumb to what was obvious in the situation, but played from a deeper level, they came out with something entirely new and liberating. But your scripts expose intimacies, privacies, in a way that's very tense as far as the audience is concerned. It's why European filmmakers, especially, look at your films as real landmarks in film history. You let the act of performance, on the set, determine a great deal, but do you write the script as intuitively as you direct? When I interviewed Gena, she told me there were no improvised lines at all in *Woman*.

Cassavetes: The preparations for the scripts I've written are really long, hard, boring, intense studies. I don't just enter into a film and say, "That's the film we're going to do." I think, "Why make it?" For a long time. I think, "Well, could the people be themselves, does this really happen to people, do they really dream this, do they think this?"

In replacing narrative, you need an idea. And the idea in *Woman Under the Influence* was, could love exist. Then, in 1974, '75. Could it exist? Society had already changed. Is it possible that two people could really be in love with each other under the conditions of the new world, where love is really a sideline? It's a word. And it's even offensive—like "art" in Los Angeles.

So that was interesting to see, whether that could be done. And it's impossible to determine the result when you start. You *know* it's going to be painful, to begin with, but you hope that the love will be strong enough that you can take the picture as far as it has to go. The adventure of making films is to say, "Can we do it? I mean, is it possible to do it?"

Ventura: The process of "doing it" is getting more and more interminable. What would you say to a young director who asks you, "What's the most important thing I should think about?"

Cassavetes: I would probably say, "Love the artists, and—screw the rest of the people."

Ventura: Would you say the same thing to an actor?

Cassavetes: An actor? Performing artists are different from anybody. They get up there, and they're all alone. And the only thing they have is the material to support them. And in between times a person says, "I don't like what you did. Perhaps if you did *this*, it might be better." And no matter how you say that, it always comes out just as crudely as that. And the actor's feeling is, "You don't like the way I sat? I've been sitting down that way all my life! Stay out of my life! Stay out of my guts. I don't need you around."

It's a very hard job, being an actor. Because the camera slate comes down in front of your face in the movies, and someone says to you in essence, "Be big, now!" Because after they finish powdering you, and dusting you, and messing with your hair, and throwing you in front of the camera, and then there's the tension, "QUIET now! It's a long scene!" And you're standing there with a bunch of strangers that you have nothing in common with, whom you're supposed to love or hate, and with a bunch of words that you don't really want to say. And a different kind of acting is born of that, and that is a professionalism, a professional, theatrical kind of acting, which all actors have done. But in films like Mazursky's or mine, we have a different view of what you are.

Ventura: To say the least, it's hard to get that view across in this business.
Cassavetes: The business stinks. It always has. It's always been a crappy business with crappy people in it. *I'm* one of those crappy people, too. I'm one of them! I negotiate for anything I can get. And take advantage. Just the way everybody else does. I'm just as dumb as anybody else. I think that we're all barbarians, basically. Occasionally, we come up with an idea—like, we pray for rain and it rains. We think that's gonna do it.

Ventura: You don't make films as though you think people are all barbarians.
Cassavetes: I don't see anything wrong with barbarians. I *don't* really see anything wrong with barbarians. I mean, occasionally we feel poetic. I've seen a lot of drunken sailors. But most of the time it's just dog eat dog—our truth is what's convenient for us. All of us. What's wrong with that? You can't be an idealist twenty-four hours a day. You've got to pick something that's important to you and stick with it. The rest of it is your own personality, saying, "Shithead, go ahead! But you're gonna suffer for it!"

But if you find something you like to do, you think that's a beautiful thing. I like to act in films, I like to shoot 'em, I like to direct 'em, I like to be around them, I like the smell of it, I like the feel of it, and it's something I respect. A lot. It doesn't make any difference whether it's a crappy film or a good film. Anybody who can make a film, I already love—but I feel sorry for them if they didn't put any *thoughts* in it. 'Cause then they missed the boat.

There is no great film. There's just something that touches you for a moment. And the only mistake the barbarians, which is us, make, is not giving people hope. That they could have that moment in the sun.

Retracing the Stream of Love

Richard Combs / 1984

From *Monthly Film Bulletin* 51(603) (April 1984): 109–10. Reprinted by permission of the British Film Institute.

John Cassavetes follows a collaboration back to its source. . . .

Families

John Cassavetes: Ted Allan and I have been working on *Love Streams* as a project for about ten years now, on and off. It's been simplified and simplified until now it's really complicated because it's so simple. Actually, the play of *Love Streams* was first put on in London, at which time it was called *I've Seen You Cut Lemons*. I thought it was a wonderful story, but when Ted asked me if I would do it, I said, well, I don't like the man, he just sits there and listens to this woman raving on for a long time. But when we started working on it as a film, bringing in all those references to other characters, he thought this opened it up so beautifully that he rewrote it as a play which became *Love Streams*.

We staged it in Los Angeles, in a group of three plays which included another one of Ted's, *The Third Day Comes*, which is the beginning of *Love Streams*, it shows you these characters as kids and how they came to be this way. The setting of *Love Streams* was still London, it was a British story, although for the film we changed it to Los Angeles, because it was shot in our house and that would hardly be London. Actually, the play was a bit different in that it was basically a comedy. Jon Voight played in it with Gena, and he has a wonderful sense of the ridiculous in comedy, his basic instincts are absolutely humorous. I was so angry with Jon when he decided not to do the movie. We were two weeks away from shooting, and there was no way I was going to let the whole production fall apart, so I did it, but reluctantly. A lot of things were redone, but I'm nowhere near Jon's disposition or personality. Apart from the fact that he and Gena look so much alike. They're both blond, they look like they could come from the same family.

A lot of Ted's work is autobiographical, which is what I find makes it interesting. It also makes it easier for him to contend with me, because he can always say either that he's having another seizure or that this is a real story and what do I know about it. For years, in our work, he had talked about his father. They had had a terrible split, and in working on the script we had awful battles because of this difference in background. My family and I were very friendly, and Ted, who is a mature man, was still trapped by this memory of his father. So the play was a retracing of his footsteps, because he was really the Robert Harmon character. He went back and wrote *The Third Day Comes* when he was in hospital and he thought he was going to die. It's a play about his father, which I had been encouraging him to write for years. It's the story of his early life in Montreal, with his sister and his family, and you see the beginnings of this writer and his relationship with his sister.

We hope to do it as a film next year, which is a little backwards. But it is such a devastatingly non-commercial film that it is very difficult to walk up to people and say, look, this film is not going to make any money but it's quite beautiful, and we love it. Cannon has agreed to make it. At first, Menahem Golan said, why would I want to make a picture that's not going to make any money, we're not in the business of throwing away money. So I told him the story and he started becoming emotional about it. He said no, it won't make any money, but we must do it. It will be a memory. You see them as children, when they break away from the tradition of the family. And you see the emotions grow stronger in that breaking away, through individuality and leaping out into the street. Which I consider to be less warm, certainly, than the family tradition.

I was attracted to Ted through friendship and work, and through the fact of his enormous obsession with family and loss and pain. I'm really interested in his stories (he also wrote *Lies My Father Told Me*) because the roots of people have somehow been lost and shunted aside, particularly in America. Living is kids— it's a very inarticulate thing, but it's something that we felt when we were doing the film and we'd say, oh yes, we have to have a kid here. Robert Harmon has no concept of children, he hasn't seen his son since he was born, and he doesn't know how to deal with somebody who loves him. He goes out with a bunch of dames, and gets drunk, and makes bargains with the boy as if he's buying off one of his girls. I don't think he's cruel, he's just ignorant. But he has an affinity with having children around, with having people live in the house like a family, even though they're rent-a-people. He tries to simulate some sort of a family style of living, which is totally made up.

The screw-up comes from the loss of family, we feel, from not taking the good and irritating parts of family and putting them together. It's a universal subject, something that everyone goes through, the parents' discovery and the discovery of parents. I'm not a young man and I treasure the memory of my mother and father. They offer me a great deal of incentive for living, because of the way they conducted the family and orchestrated our lives. I haven't yet been able to deal with my own family in my work. It's just too close, and I'm confused enough by life in general. I have such admiration for people who can recount their lives in autobiography, because the connections are so complicated. I would never be able to straighten it out. Long after I was dead, I'd have to have some script, or scroll, to be working on up there, or down there, or wherever.

Fortunes

Love Streams is probably much more formal than my other films. Everyone complained for so long about us being informal that I thought maybe we'd do a formal film. In a way, it's just a mechanic of the fact that nothing is happening. You can't have it be goulash and have nothing happening. It just singles itself out from moment to moment, when somebody is in a place where nothing is going on. All of a sudden you realize that these people really are in solitude. It's something you feel if you live in California. You feel that life is really a dream. Nothing can bother you. Even the hospitals are so enormous and splendiferous that you feel you're in a social club. You're dying and people are coming to visit you in the emergency ward, bringing drinks and beautiful women.

Los Angeles is quite an empty place. It's a series of houses, many people just living with a small coterie of friends like in a tiny village. You see the same people and you grow old before you know it because the sun is the same every day. People entertain in their homes and they work for a major studio—it's just like a small town with one factory. I find it very pleasant to work there, because actors and cameramen and writers don't have the feeling that anything can transpire there. So they're very anxious to work, they're very happy to do little theatre all the time. They don't want to leave there because that's where the financial work is, but you'll find great Hollywood stars going out and working in waiver productions for nothing, simply because that's what they need to feel alive. And you can do serious work in Los Angeles, whereas New York is such a diversion in itself. I don't like to work in New York, because it's too exciting. We know Los Angeles well. There's a downtown and there's a life there—you just have to find it.

I think, really, that it's vastly unimportant whether people have money or not. If they don't have money, they live a different kind of creative life; if they do have money, they struggle *for* a creative life. That's what I feel about loneliness, too. If you don't have any tie to yourself, then you seek to be alone. And that is maybe more irritating, funnier, lighter, but somehow more proper than to be alone, not out of choice, and to seek companionship and family. Certainly in *Love Streams* nothing is sad except the fact that they're alone, they're the only two people left in their family. The fact that they don't have a financial problem at the moment is because they deem that important—not to have a financial problem—to the exclusion of many other things. Basically, I think that rich people are the real children. If we live in a materialistic world, then my view is that they have nothing if they have nothing. It's just a little powder to put on people, a pill to pop, a momentary diversion. It helps to pay the bills, and once you're past that plateau, everything else is the same. Friendships are harder to come by for rich people, and they're more limited. I think it's very important that rich people and poor people realize that they have the same problems, it's just that somebody on the street made some money. . . .

Fantasies

I find that most people are the same. I don't know about the rest of the world; through Gena, who is from the Midwest and whose family is from the South, I was able to meet relatives and get to know them on a different level than just walking around and saying, hey, I know the South, I know the Midwest, and I know the North. You really have to be with people and understand them. I've used most of our family and relatives in our films, and I don't think you get to know anybody unless you work with them. You see people's personalities emerge as very individual, and they're surprising. Some people want something out of life, and some people just get very earthy. And some people get very nervous. But most people are actors, and once they begin acting all that pretense disappears. They become very articulate about what they really want if you give them an opportunity.

It's pain. We love pain. I think all good humor comes out of pain, and all good works come out of the understanding that life is painful. The modern world denies this, but it's a normal thing, it's nothing spectacular. I see young people turning away from pain—like an older person would turn away, because he's had enough—when to overcome it is a glorious part of life. I just hope our films keep on opening up a dark pathway for young people. We really make them for the young, we don't make them for older people. Old people know all that stuff. Maybe for them it is defined a little more clearly, but for young people it's a mystery. We hope we don't make lecture films. But by seeing people who have lived a little bit, maybe they'll see in their own lives that it never changes. When I'm told that our films are painful, I think, oh God, I know real pain. We soften our pictures so tremendously. We make them almost romantic fantasies, and just barely touch on these things in a more idealistic way than other people do.

The Lost Interview: John Cassavetes

Joe Leydon / 1985

From *MovieMaker, The Art and Business of Making Movies* (online), January 29, 2009.
Reprinted by permission of Joe Leydon.

Author's Note: Back in 1985, I wrote the interview—greatly expanded from a piece I originally wrote as film critic for the Houston Post—*as a spec freelance article. At the time, unfortunately, no one was buying what I was selling. One editor informed me that Cassavetes was "yesterday's news," while another admitted to actively disliking the man's work. So I consigned the manuscript to my archives, where it remained until I unearthed it, and slightly revised it, as a memorial tribute to mark the twentieth anniversary of John Cassavetes's death.*

Here's the scene. It is early 1985 and John Cassavetes, somehow both casual and intense, sits at a cluttered desk in his office at Burbank Studios, surrounded by blown-up stills from his current effort, *Big Trouble*. The movie, a comedy now in post-production, is planned as a major summer release by Columbia Pictures. Its stars, many of them in photos surrounding Cassavetes's desk, include Alan Arkin, Peter Falk, Beverly D'Angelo, Charles Durning, and Robert Stack. Cassavetes is smiling, clearly enjoying himself. The assistants who drift in and out of his office with reports on looping and editing are smiling. And, if you can believe the advance word dribbling in from studio people who have seen the rushes, Columbia is smiling a great big corporate smile.

What is wrong with this picture?

After all, this is John Cassavetes, the first Angry Young Man of cinema, the gray eminence of American independent moviemakers, a virtual deity to every film school student who dreams of making a splash outside the Hollywood mainstream. Here is the creator of such rough-edged, defiantly unpolished, semi-improvised dramas as *A Woman Under the Influence* (1974), *Opening Night* (1977), and *Love Streams* (1984), pictures in which life is served up like steak tartare: Raw and not appealing to every taste.

This is the maverick director who never walks near a studio backlot, except when he takes an acting job to supplement his meager production budgets. Here is the iconoclast who, along with his wife and frequent star, Gena Rowlands, has gone deeply into debt many times, to the point of mortgaging his West Coast home, to pay for his handmade projects.

Now this same man is wrapping up work on a Hollywood comedy. No kidding.

As he drives to the St. Moritz in Studio City, seeking a break from post-production and a quiet place to talk, Cassavetes grins wolfishly as he considers his atypical assignment as a Hollywood director for hire. "Well," he begins, dividing his gaze between the windshield and his passenger, "Peter Falk is a real good friend, for one thing. They called me in the middle of the night and said, 'How would you like to do this? The producer-writer-director [Andrew Bergman] is exhausted. He finds it too much for him to do all these things. It will be kind of fun if you come on for five weeks and have a good time with Peter and everybody.' And I said yes immediately, because I wasn't doing anything else.

"But as it's turned out," the legendary indie adds as he pauses for a traffic light, "this is my seventh month. It's a lot more difficult than I thought it would be."

But not as difficult as convincing Columbia you were the man for the job, right? Not really, Cassavetes replies. He has worked in the past with the studio, which released his movies *Husbands* (1970) and *Gloria* (1980). Despite all the stories of his epic battles against the Hollywood system, he has more than his fair share of supporters and admirers among the production powers that be.

"Oddly enough," he says, "I grew up with most of the people who are heads of studios. And while they don't like my kinds of films, when I make 'em, I really never had too much trouble getting a job in a more commercial area. I just don't want that, usually.

"But this appealed to me," he continues. "I thought it'd be fun. I've never done a comedy before. In fact, they were a little shaken when I told the actors, 'Look, I've never done comedy before—so let's cut all the laughs out.' I said, 'Laughs are easy to come by. Let's push the story.'"

Bergman's original screenplay was sort of a comic take on *Double Indemnity*, with Alan Arkin as a hard-working insurance salesman drawn into a high-stakes scam by a brassy femme fatale (D'Angelo) and her con man "husband" (Falk). Hoping to collect on a special clause in an accidental death policy, the plotters match wits with a straight-laced, ultraconservative insurance executive played by Eliot Ness himself, Robert Stack.

"So far," Cassavetes says as the restaurant comes into view, "I think the studio likes the picture a lot, oddly enough. I think they have a lot of respect for me. And I have a lot of respect for them in that they've gone along with me. They're rooting for me to be able to accomplish this.

"I'm not saying it's not dangerous. It is dangerous, because I'm greedy. I don't want a film that could be my last film—as all films could be—that would be something that could be pigeonholed. I want it to be funny, but I want it to be truly funny. I want it to be something that could happen to somebody."

Could *Big Trouble* really be Cassavetes's swan song as a director? The very idea brings a slight chill to the conversation, causing a frisson that cannot be blamed on a blast of air conditioning as we enter the St. Moritz. Cassavetes remains jocular while we're at the bar, speaking with mock gravity about the car we left outside with a parking attendant. ("I don't know if this place really does have valet parking. Maybe that was just some guy who took my keys . . .") Then he orders a Coca-Cola, instead of the expected pre-lunch cocktail. (*This is in deference to the cirrhosis that already has ravaged his liver and bloated his stomach, and will kill him four years hence. —JL*)

It's spooky: From some angles, Cassavetes's gaunt face evokes memories of the late John Marley, who starred in *Faces* (1968). Later, after we return to Burbank, he will politely but firmly decline when I ask to take a photo. Even spookier: The sudden intimation of mortality during a pleasant conversation—it's like something out of one of the director's movies.

Cassavetes appears both amused and intrigued when I mention my curiosity about a recurring motif in his work: The unexpected, frightening realization that life is short and fragile. "You mean, how do I look at the death sentence that's been given all of us? Well, yeah, I think that's what good drama is made of: Life and death. I mean, if it isn't life and death, it's a comedy. Everything passionate, everything to do with love and hate, anything that is important, has to do with someone saying, 'Hey, this is the last time. This is it, right now, this day that we're living is the time.'

"I guess I'm colored by the fact that, when you're making films, me and all the other people working on it work like it's the last time, the last film, like there is no other film. So I guess the characters become implanted with that, too. In the writing and in the execution. It's the last time, and we might as well live, because we don't have much of an alternative.

"I think you feel mortality more when you're most alive, really. Because that's when you don't want anything to happen to you. When you're depressed, let's face it, you don't really care about death that much. You think, 'Listen, that might be a solution to my problems.' But if you're having a wonderful time, if you're feeling life and it's really grappling with you, then you get worried. It's like a rich man being afraid of being robbed. A poor man is not so afraid of being robbed—unless, of course, it's payday. But the day after, you don't care anymore."

Cassavetes cares very much about *Big Trouble*, in large part because it really could be his last film. One moment, he indicates as much. The next moment, however, he contradicts himself: "I could do another movie, easy." It all depends on his health, he says.

"With this kind of disease, you don't know whether the liver regenerates or it doesn't."

Is it difficult, even after making so many movies about facing up to mortality, for Cassavetes to consider the possibility of his own death?

"Well, emotionally, as I look at it, I'm not aware of anything that's wrong with me. I guess I can't cope very well with things that mean a lot to me—like most people. It comes out in different reactions. But I can never face anything that I don't want to happen. I'll fight to the death, you know. And I think there have been certain things in the past number of years—well, I wasn't aware that they were happening, or that they meant that much to me, but they evidently did. They're personal things; I don't want to discuss them with myself, why should I talk about them with you?"

Cassavetes is smiling as he speaks, but there is a slight edge to his voice. "That's fair," I reply. "I'm conducting an interview, not a psychiatric session."

"Well you're doing both," he retorts, exploding into laughter, vigorously slapping the table where my tape recorder is whirring. "But, seriously, they were personal things. I don't cope well with the loss of people I love and things like that. I went through a really terrible manic period and I think my health broke down on me. So I'm taking better care of myself. Gena is insisting that the strong body I've been given should be cared for a bit more. I don't know. I guess other people wouldn't think about it as much, but I rest when I can."

Faced with his serious ailment, Cassavetes's reaction is one of annoyance, not fear. "Not having as much energy is very frustrating. I used to have enormous energy and could accomplish a great deal. Now it takes me a longer period of time to accomplish what I could accomplish in a very, very short time. Outside of that—the rest of it—well, that's life."

The hard-scrabble days of Cassavetes's early directing career were long behind him. But he vividly recalls the period in the late 1950s and early '60s when, still young and optimistic, he tried to revolutionize the art of moviemaking in America. The New York–born son of Greek immigrants, Cassavetes was profoundly influenced by his father, a Harvard-educated businessman who made and lost millions. "My father was a gambler because he had to be," Cassavetes notes. "From that point of view, I'm very similar. I had to be a gambler—I had no choice. So I'd rather enjoy it, rather than think of it as something terrible or repressive. I've been selfish all my life. And the thing Gena says is, 'What I don't understand about you is that you're proud of it!'"

Legend has it that in 1959, Cassavetes actually solicited funds for his first feature, *Shadows*, on a late-night radio talk show. The legend, Cassavetes admits, is true. At the time, he recalls, he was establishing himself as an actor in live television and sharing his expertise by conducting an acting workshop in Manhattan. After supervising a particularly successful improvisational exercise, he thought of translating the classroom activity into a movie.

"So I went on this show—Jean Shepherd's *Night People*—and I said, 'Wouldn't it be wonderful if people each sent in a dollar and we'd go out and make a film?' The next day, seven thousand dollars came in, in dollar bills, and people from all over brought in equipment. It was like a miracle. So then we had to make the film.

"Of course, it cost considerably more than seven thousand dollars , but people continued to send in money. Suddenly there were people calling me up and saying, 'Well, I'm gonna put in one hundred dollars.' Hedda Hopper called me up and sent me thirty-five dollars; I thought that was very sweet. But I told her, 'Fine, I'm taking it. But you don't get a piece of the profits.'"

Shadows, a highly praised psychological drama, attracted the attention of Hollywood producers. But Cassavetes was less than pleased by the two movies he subsequently made for major studios: *Too Late Blues* (1961) and *A Child Is Waiting* (1963). Much closer to his heart is *Faces*, an ultra-low-budget, 16mm production which took four years to film and edit. (He helped finance the movie with his salaries for acting in *The Dirty Dozen*, for which he earned an Oscar nomination, and *Rosemary's Baby*.) *Faces*, a drama about the tensions of an upper-middle-class marriage, opened in 1968. Critics and audiences responded with an enthusiasm that took Cassavetes by surprise.

"I was young," he recalls, "but not that young. We sat around, [producer] Sam Shaw and me, and some of the reviews came in. And they were very important to us, because this was a picture that counted on the press. So we were looking at them. And then we started laughing, 'cause the reviews were so good. I remember one that Roger Ebert happened to write. Sam and I laughed and laughed and laughed and laughed. Sam started pointing at me, I started pointing at the paper and we were laughing. We weren't laughing at Ebert, but what he said seemed so excessive in praise."

Not all of Cassavetes's movies were met with such a reception. "A couple of pictures later," Cassavetes recalls, "Ebert rapped me. My first thought was, 'Where's that first review? Why is he saying I'm such a bad director after this excessive thing? Maybe he's trying to balance it?'

"I think that all artists, in some strange kind of sick way, pay more attention to the bad reviews. But with me, it's like I'm somebody who built a car by hand. Somebody takes a ride in a factory-built car and gives that car a good review. Then he rides in our hand-built car that we spent four years on and says, 'Well, it's rough, the shift doesn't work.' I wanna say, 'Yeah, but what about the car?'"

Remember: It's early 1985 and Cassavetes has been polarizing critics and audiences for more than fifteen years. *Husbands* and *A Woman Under the Influence*, two brilliant movies that are arguably his best, were very well received. (Cassavetes himself was a Best Director contender for *A Woman Under the Influence* and Rowlands was Oscar-nominated as Best Actress.) But *Minnie and Moskowitz*, *The Killing of a Chinese Bookie*, *Opening Night*, *Gloria*, and *Love Streams* sharply divided critics and failed to attract large audiences.

Still, Cassavetes had managed to maintain his drive and enthusiasm—as well as his strong working relationship with his wife of thirty-one years. "Gena's point of view is totally different from mine," he laughs. "But I think that's great. God, if we agreed on everything—can you imagine? Just see us, walking through life, and we're getting a little older, and people say, 'Oh, they're just alike! They agree on everything! If she says 'blue,' he says 'blue.' They really are together!'

"Well, if Gena says 'green,' I say 'red!' If I say 'red,' she says 'blue.' It's like clockwork! We're totally, diametrically opposed on everything. I admire the hell out of her, because this has led me into at least an understanding of the way a person with a totally different background, a totally different cultural understanding of life, feels and thinks. The beauty of working with her is that I think she's a great actress. I think anybody working with her would know it."

Trouble is, in 1985, some of her best work isn't easily available for public scrutiny. *Minnie and Moskowitz*, which was financed by Universal Pictures, occasionally pops up on late-night TV. *Gloria*, made for Columbia, is available on VHS. But the movies Cassavetes financed on his own are rarely revived—mainly because he seldom permits them to be shown anywhere but museums and film festivals. Our conversation is timed to a retrospective of his work at the Museum of Fine Arts, Houston.

"You know, through the years we financed our own films. And at a certain point, there was a stop put on that by people just not buying them. For any reason. So now, later on, when people come over and say, 'Oh, we'll give you a dollar for the film,' well, I'd really rather show them in museums for people. I've already taken a tremendous financial loss."

So, at fifty-five, is Cassavetes still a maverick?

The question elicits a melancholy smile. Cassavetes stares at his soft drink for a moment as he calmly considers his answer. "People used to love to call me a maverick because I had a big mouth and I'd say, 'That bum!' or something like that when I was young. Mainly because I believed it and I didn't know there was anybody's pain connected to the business. I was so young, I didn't feel any pain. I just thought, 'Why don't they do some exciting, venturesome things? Why are they just sitting there, doing these dull pictures that have already been done many,

many times and calling them exciting? That's a lie. They're not exciting. Exciting is an experiment.'

"Now, from the point of view of a guy in his twenties, that was true. But when I look back on it, I think, 'Yes, that man was a maverick. But . . .'"

His words trail off into weak laughter.

"That reputation keeps with you through the years. Once the press calls you a maverick, it stays in their files. I'll be dead five years and they'll still be saying, 'That maverick son-of-a-bitch, he's off in Colorado, making a movie.' As if they really cared.

"You know, in this business, it's all jealousy. I mean, this is the dumbest business I've ever seen in my life. If somebody gets married, they say, 'It'll never work.' If somebody gets divorced, they say, 'Good. I'll give you my lawyer.' If somebody loses a job, everyone will call him—to gloat. They'll discuss it, they'll be happy, they'll have parties. I don't understand how people who see each other all the time, and are friends, can be so happy about each other's demise.

"I think people—studio executives and filmmakers—should hate each other openly and save a lot of trouble. It's like me and actors. I never get along with actors, not on the level of friendship, because I don't believe in it—only on a creative level. Now, through a period of years, Peter Falk and I have become very good friends, as have Ben Gazzara and I. But only after a period of years. That friendship came out of working on *Husbands* together and the success that came out of that and a lot of other films, too. Sometimes we've been successful and sometimes we've been unsuccessful. The creative part of it has always been successful. That's been the bargain of it, our relationship.

"But I'm sure that the moment I was no longer interested in anything artistic, Peter would not be my friend anymore, and that would be fair game. I probably wouldn't be his friend, either, if I weren't interested in art."

Even so, the opportunity to work with Falk was the primary enticement when Cassavetes was offered *Big Trouble*. Stepping in at the last minute to direct someone else's script is usually not his style. But he's tried it and he likes it.

"I've thought about it awhile," he says, "and I think that's the best way to come into a picture. You don't have to hunt locations, you don't have to go through all the hassles, you don't have to say, 'This isn't right, that isn't right.'"

Cassavetes pauses and takes another sip of his drink.

"It's been a lot of trouble," he says, "but I've enjoyed it."

Making *Big Trouble*?

"No," he says, smiling once again. "I meant my whole life."

Postscript: *Big Trouble* was spottily released—dumped, really—by Columbia in the spring of 1986. Reviews were mixed, although Vincent Canby of the *New York*

Times, not always a fan of the moviemaker, wrote that it was "great seeing Mr. Cassavetes direct a heedless comedy that appears to be a result of special friendships, rather than (like *Husbands*) an exhausting analysis of them. He can be a very funny man."

Cassavetes never directed another feature film. He died on February 3, 1989, at age fifty-nine. His children, son Nick (*The Notebook*) and daughters Xan (*Z Channel: A Magnificent Obsession*) and Zoe (*Broken English*), have all continued their father's work behind the camera, on many occasions with their mother in a starring role.

Resources

AuWerter, Russ. "Editing the Personal Feature—John Cassavetes' *Husbands*." *Cinemeditor*, Fall 1969.

Barclay, Dolores. "John Cassavetes Gets His Reward." *Los Angeles Times*, July 8, 1980.

Benson, Sheila. "Cassavetes Left His Imprint on a Generation of Film Makers." *Los Angeles Times*, February 6, 1989.

Bosworth, Patricia. "Cassavetes: Why Do Marriages Go Sour?" *New York Times*, December 1, 1968.

Calio, Jim. "Mavericks John Cassavetes and Gena Rowlands Make Movies the Hard Way—with Their Own Money." *People*, October 8, 1984.

Cameron, Sue. "John Cassavetes Talks It Up for the Star System." *Hollywood Reporter*, December 24, 1970.

Carney, Ray. *Cassavetes on Cassavetes*. London: Faber and Faber, 2001.

Carney, Ray. *The Films of John Cassavetes: Pragmatism, Modernism, and the Movies*. New York: Cambridge University Press, 1994.

Carroll, Kathleen. "Cassavetes—Filming 'Em Where They Live." *New York Daily News*, November 3, 1974.

Cassavetes, John. "And the Pursuit of Happiness." *Films and Filming*, February 1961.

Cassavetes, John. "How Love and Life Mingle on Film." *New York Times*, August 19, 1984.

Cassavetes, John. "Letters to the Editors: 'Shadows,' cont." *Village Voice*, December 16, 1959.

"Cassavetes Strives for New Concept and Paramount Completely Sympatico." *Variety*, February 8, 1961.

Champlain, Charles. "Still a Maverick Movie Maker." *Los Angeles Times*, August 27, 1984.

Charity, Tom. *John Cassavetes: Lifeworks*. New York: Omnibus Press, 2001.

Ciment, Michel, and Michael Henry. "An Interview with John Cassavetes." *Positif*, no. 180 (April 1976).

Crittenden, John. "Directed by John Casssavetes and Starring Gena Rowlands." *Sunday Record* (Bergen County, NJ), October 20, 1974.

Dargis, Manohla. "John Cassavetes, Laughing Last." *New York Times*, September 26, 2004.

"Dear Boss: I'm Sorry I Couldn't Interview Gena . . . but John Cassavetes Could." *New York Times (Sunday)*, February 13, 1972.

Degener, David. "Director Under the Influence." *Film Quarterly*, Winter 1975–76.

Denis, Christopher Paul. "Direct It: John Cassavetes." *Video Review*, November 1985, p. 81.

"The Faces of the Husbands." *New Yorker*, March 15, 1969.

Fine, Marshall. *Accidental Genius: How John Cassavetes Invented the American Independent Film*. New York: Miramax Books/Hyperion, 2005.

Galligan, David. "Competitive Cassavetes." *Hollywood Dramalogue*, October 7–13, 1982.

"Gena and John Cassavetes Talk about Their 'Faces.' Abe Greenberg's Voice of Hollywood." *Hollywood Citizen News*, December 11, 1968.

Gibbs, Patrick. "How *Shadows* Was Born." *Daily Telegraph*, October 15, 1960.

Gosling, Nigel. "This Film Called *Shadows*." *Observer*, August 7, 1960.

Gross, Larry. "John Cassavetes: *A Woman Under the Influence*." *Millimeter*, March 1975.

Haskell, Molly. "Three Husbands Hold Court." *Show*, September 1969,

Haun, Harry. "The Case on Cassavetes." *New York Daily News*, April 30, 1991.

Hays, Matthew. "Gena on John." *Montreal Mirror*, February 7, 2002.

Hopper, Hedda. "Take It from Gena—It's a Man's World." *Los Angeles Times*, September 23, 1962.

Hyams, Joe. "Picture of Cassavetes Biting the 'Free Hand.'" *New York Herald Tribune*, March 12, 1961.

"Interview Express . . . avec John Cassavetes." *Ecran*, 15 mai 1976.

Jacobs, Diane. *Hollywood Renaissance: Altman, Cassavetes, Coppola, Mazursky, Scorsese and Others*. New York: A.S. Barnes & Co., 1977.

"John Cassavetes." *Film Quarterly*, Spring 1961.

"John Cassavetes: Master of Poetic Confusion." *American Film*, May 1989.

"John Cassavetes." *New York Sunday News*, May 20, 1979.

"John Cassavetes." *Sight and Sound*, Summer, 1961.

"John Cassavetes: What's a Good Marriage Without a Good Fight?" *Coronet*, November 1969.

Johnson, Erskine. "'Nothing' Is Film's Synopsis." *Los Angeles Mirror*, March 8, 1961.

Kelley, Bill. "OK, Now, Does Everyone Know Who John Cassavetes Is?" *Sarasota Herald-Tribune*, April 6, 2001.

Knapp, Dan. "Cassavetes' Personal Rebellion." *Los Angeles Times*, November 9, 1969.

Kouvaros, George. *Where Does It Happen? John Cassavetes and Cinema at the Break-ing Point*. Minneapolis, MN: University of Minnesota Press, 2004.

Krebs, Albin. "John Cassavetes, Major Director in U.S. Cinema Verité, Dies at 59." *New York Times*, February 4, 1989.

Labarthe, Andre S. "A Way of Life: An Interview with John Cassavetes." *Evergreen Review*, January 1971.

Lardeau, Yann. "Le bal des vauriens." *Cahiers du cinéma*, juin 1978.

Lardine, Bob. "Acting Independently, John Cassavetes Travels a Lonely Road in Meeting Today's Problems." *New York Sunday News*, September 21, 1969.

Lefèvre, Raymond. "John Cassavetes: Une camera sue le qui-vive." *Cinéma*, fevrier 1977.

Letter to the Editor by John Cassavetes. *Village Voice*, December 16, 1959.

Lewis, Brent. "Cassavetes Recalled." *Films and Filming*, April 1989.

Linderman, Lawrence. "The *Playboy* Interview: John Cassavetes." *Playboy*, July 1971.

Linehan, Gary. "Cassavetes Returns to Director's Chair in Cannon Production of *Love Streams*." *On Location*, January 1984.

Maychick, Diana. "Pitch and Roll on 'Tempest' Set." *New York Post*, August 12, 1982.

McNally, Judith. "*A Woman Under the Influence*: An Interview with John Cassa-vetes." *Filmmakers Newsletter*, January 1975.

Mekas, Jonas. "Movie Journal." *Village Voice*, December 23, 1971.

Mekas, Jonas. "Movie Journal." *Village Voice*, January 27, 1960.

Michelson, Herb. "*Streams* Withheld from Frisco Fest; Cassavetes Blames Distri-bution." *Variety*, April 25, 1984.

"'Minnie and Moskowitz' Is a Cassavetes Family Affair." *New York Sunday News*, December 19, 1971.

Nevers, Camille. "Cassavetes: *Shadows* and *Faces*." *Cahiers du cinéma*, mars 1992.

O'Brian, Jack. "Cassavetes Prepared Long for Break." *New York Journal American*, November 9, 1955.

Oral History Research Office, Columbia University. "John Cassavetes." New York, Spring 1959.

"Out of the Shadows." *Newsweek*, November 7, 1960.

Pasquariello, Nicholas. "John Cassavetes: I Really Like What I Do." *Weekly Califor-nian*, April 18–25, 1975.

Pollack, Dale. "Cassavetes: Sunshine Amid a Midlife Tempest." *Los Angeles Times*, August 12, 1982.

Quinn, Frank. "Cassavetes in New York." *New York Mirror*, March 16, 1958.

Quinn, Frank. "John Cassavetes Wants Wife to Star." *Sunday Mirror*, April 29, 1956.

Roberts, Meade. "A Recollection of Cassavetes." *Hollywood*, December 1990–January 1991.

Ross, Alexander. "John Cassavetes: The Actor Who Taught Hollywood How to Make Films." *Macleans*, May 1969.

Ross, Don. "John Cassavetes, Delinquent." *New York Herald Tribune*, January 20, 1957.

Salmaggi, Bob. "John Cassavetes: A Change of Heart." *New York Herald Tribune*, August 2, 1959.

Scheuer, Philip K. "Does Flood of Improvisations Mean New Wave in Films?" *Los Angeles Times*, May 21, 1961.

Schreger, Charles. "Cassavetes: Making of a Movie Maker." *Los Angeles Times*, September 16, 1980.

Scott, Vernon. "Actor Sounds Off—on Other Actors." *Los Angeles Herald Examiner*, February 13, 1968.

Setlowe, Rick. "Cassavetes Retrospective Perks Up San Francisco Film Festival." *Variety*, October 28, 1970.

Simon, Francesca. "Inside the Eye of the Story: John Cassavetes Talks up the Magic of 'Tempest.'" *Los Angeles Herald Examiner*, August 27, 1982.

Simsolo, Noël. "Note sur le cinema de John Cassavetes." *Cahiers du cinéma*, mai 1978.

Skolsky, Sidney. "Tintypes: John Cassavetes." *New York Post*, July 29, 1967.

Smith, Cecil. "Actor Directs No-Script Film." *Los Angeles Times*, January 31, 1960.

Stevenson, James. "John Cassavetes: Film's Bad Boy." *Film Comment*, January–February 1980.

Topor, Tom. "Cassavetes Pleased with Museum Exhibit." *New York Post*, June 20, 1980.

Torre, Marie. "Cassavetes Hits Agency's Stand on Scripts." *Beverly Hills Citizen*, December 10, 1959.

"Une manière de vivre: entretien." *Cahiers du cinéma*, octobre 1968.

Ventura, Michael. *Cassavetes Directs: John Cassavetes and the Making of "Love Streams."* Harpenden, UK: Kamera Books, 2007.

Ventura, Michael. "Cassavetes: Show Me the Magic." *LA Weekly*, August 20–26, 1982.

Ventura, Michael. "John Cassavetes' Last Scene." *Austin Chronicle*, March 8, 2002.

Ventura, Michael. "Remembrance." *Sight and Sound*, November 1991.

Ventura, Michael. "Zen and the Art of John Cassavetes." *LA Weekly*, September 21–27, 1984.

Viera, Martin. "Cassavetes' Working Methods: Interviews with Al Ruban and Seymour Cassel." *Post Script*, March 1988.

Films

Five Films by John Cassavetes. Criterion Collection [DVD], 2004.

John Cassavetes: To Risk Everything to Express It All. Kultur Films, Inc., 1999.

Kiselyak, Charles, *A Constant Forge: The Life and Art of John Cassavetes*. 2000.

Powell, Tristram. *The Making of "Husbands."* Omnibus, BBC, 1970.

Ventura, Michael. *I'm Almost Not Crazy: John Cassavetes—The Man and His Work*. Cannon Films, 1984.

Index

CPSIA information can be obtained at www.ICGtesting.com
Printed in the USA
BVOW08*2057010716

454279BV00002B/2/P